The Moscow Summit, 1988

The Moscow Summit, 1988

Reagan and Gorbachev in Negotiation

Joseph G. Whelan

Westview Press
BOULDER, SAN FRANCISCO, & OXFORD

To the memory of the late Sergius Yakobson and Leon M. Herman, senior specialists in Soviet affairs, long-time personal friends, professional colleagues, and mentors at the Congressional Research Service of the Library of Congress

Westview Special Studies in International Relations

This Westview softcover edition is printed on acid-free paper and bound in library-quality, coated covers that carry the highest rating of the National Association of State Textbook Administrators, in consultation with the Association of American Publishers and the Book Manufacturers' Institute.

Published in 1990 in the United States of America by Westview Press, Inc., 5500 Central Avenue, Boulder, Colorado 80301, and in the United Kingdom by Westview Press, Inc., 36 Lonsdale Road, Summertown, Oxford OX2 7EW

Library of Congress Cataloging-in-Publication Data
Whelan, Joseph G.
  The Moscow Summit, 1988 : Reagan and Gorbachev in negotiation /
Joseph G. Whelan.
    p. cm. — (Westview special studies in international
relations)
  Includes bibliographical references.
  ISBN 0-8133-7929-6
  1. United States — Foreign relations — Soviet Union. 2. Soviet
Union — Foreign relations — United States. 3. Summit meetings —
Russian S.F.S.R. — Moscow. 4. Visits of state — Soviet Union.
5. Reagan, Ronald — Journeys — Russian S.F.S.R. — Moscow.
6. Gorbachev, Mikhail Sergeevich, 1931–   . I. Title. II. Series.
E183.8.S65W469   1990
327.73047 — dc20   89-77270
                                                                        CIP

Printed and bound in the United States of America

 The paper used in this publication meets the requirements
of the American National Standard for Permanence of Paper
for Printed Library Materials Z39.48-1984.

10   9   8   7   6   5   4   3   2   1

Contents

Preface

PRELUDE TO MOSCOW

Two major trends dominated Soviet-American relations during the months prior to the Moscow Summit of mid-1988. The momentum of diplomatic accommodation continued along its upward swing, creating expectations of further progress in the coming superpower dialogue. But a countervailing trend persisted, notably a buildup of tensions on the human rights issue as both sides jockeyed for negotiating positions in pre-summit diplomacy, exacerbating the deeper, systemic discord that lay at the base of the relationship. The interaction of these competing forces produced a mood of positive expectation and promise as both sides prepared for the Moscow meeting, a mood generally mixed with a realistic belief that accomplishments would probably be more symbolic than substantive.

Americans approached the Moscow Summit with limited expectations. Hopes for signing a long-range strategic nuclear weapons agreement, the expected centerpiece of the summit, faded rapidly as negotiators failed to resolve their differences in last-minute efforts, though some officials seemed to hope that some progress, if not a breakthrough, could be achieved. No major changes were produced in U.S. negotiating positions after a series of pre-summit White House meetings, nor were there positive signs from the Soviet side as they held firm to their views. Since little was expected in the area of arms control, U.S. planners expected the summit to be heavy on symbolism and ceremony, and light on substance.

In contrast to U.S. limited expectations, the Soviets expressed more hope. Regular contacts were important at the summit level, they said; but they were also pressing on a number of key issues, notably the speeding up of the START negotiations and the opening of negotiations on conventional arms. For the Soviets, arms control was the primary interest.

By the time of the Moscow meeting, the over-all agenda had taken on a fairly routine pattern, given the fact that the United States did not recognize (at least formally) the supremacy of arms control; namely, arms control, regional issues, human rights and humanitarian issues, and problems in bilateral relations. Arms control, usually the de facto vital center of the concentric circle of the relationship, had top priority. Difficulties had barred the way for agreement on strategic arms on such key issues as the interpretation of the ABM Treaty and agreements on future research, testing, development and deployment of space-based ballistic missile defenses (SDI); limits on submarine-launched cruise missiles; and verification provisions. Prior to the Moscow Summit, there were no signs to encourage the belief that the broad area of disagreement over the many technical issues in strategic nuclear arms would be narrowed. Arms control was expected to be given a full airing at the Moscow Summit, but agreement, at least on the central areas of conflict in strategic nuclear weapons, was not realistically expected.

Regional issues were expected to play an important role in the Moscow Summit, particularly Soviet disengagement from Angola. Human rights was to be high on the U.S. agenda, and the President was expected to press his case for expanded human rights in the Soviet Union with renewed vigor.

Bilateral issues, a catch-all for other problems in Soviet-American relations, mostly functional, was the last category on the agenda. Many agreements were in their final stages awaiting top-level approval.

Both Gorbachev and Reagan engaged in a great deal of pre-conference maneuvering in the weeks prior to their meeting. Prominent among Gorbachev's efforts to influence the course and outcome of the upcoming summit was an extensive interview with the staff and owner of the Washington Post published on May 22, 1988. The interview, covering four printed pages of the Post, contained detailed explanations by the General Secretary of the Soviet positions to be taken at the summit. Prominent among them were his views on a strategic nuclear arms agreement as a priority issue. The interview was not only a formidable statement of Soviet expectations and goals as they entered the negotiations in Moscow, but it was also a strong counter-pressure on the U.S. negotiators to soften their stance.

In a series of statements, major speeches and an interview by Soviet journalists to be aired over Soviet television, President Reagan set forth his own expectations and goals to be achieved at Moscow. Prominent among these were his intentions of furthering the cause of human rights in the Soviet Union and establishing a "stable" and "sustainable" relationship with the Soviet Union. For the President human rights was the first item on his Moscow agenda because he saw the fulfillment of human rights linked indissolubly with the achievement of peace and security. Since differences in arms control, especially on reducing strategic offensive weapons by 50 percent, were not likely to be narrowed, his priority interest was placed on advancing the idea of human rights and expanding human contacts as a necessary corollary.

Gorbachev and Reagan also had their "hidden" agendas as they prepared to meet in Moscow. Each hoped to use the summit as a prestige-producing event to fortify his own political position at home. For Reagan there was additional incentive; namely, to end his presidency at a high point of success by negotiating a major agreement with Moscow. Both leaders, therefore, had good reason not only to meet in Moscow, but also to make their meeting a visible success.

SUMMIT MEETING IN MOSCOW

The summit meeting began on Sunday, May 29, 1988, with the President's arrival in Moscow and ended on Thursday, June 2, with his departure for Washington via London. Highlights of the first day were: the welcoming ceremony in which both leaders made it a point to stress their agenda priorities; the opening discussions in which sharp exchanges took place on the human rights issue; the President's walkabout in Arbat mall where he had his first face-to-face encounter with the Soviet people; and the setting up of working groups to deal with the problems listed on the conference agenda.

Highlights of the second day were: further discussions between the two leaders on a wide range of issues with special focus on arms control; Reagan's visit to the Danilov Monastery and meeting with dissidents at Spaso House, the U.S. Ambassador's residence, where he made a fervent plea for religious and political freedom; some progress in arms control problems at the working group level; and the formal state dinner hosted by Gorbachev at which time he elaborated on such themes as realism, dialogue and accommodation in Soviet-American relations, giving great emphasis to strategic arms control, and the President's response in which he placed special stress on his human rights agenda and the importance of a peaceful superpower dialogue.

The third day proved to be a high point of the Moscow Summit. Among the highlights were: the private meeting between Gorbachev and Reagan where the General Secretary voiced his displeasure at the slow pace of the arms control negotiations. Both leaders took an historic 20-minute stroll through Red Square, again bringing the President close to the Soviet people through television and to the few permitted in the square, but also giving the General Secretary the opportunity to press his arms control agenda to the President man-to-man. President Reagan had an important luncheon with Soviet intellectual leaders and later spoke at Moscow State University where he included in his human rights message a "lesson in American civics." The Reagans' hosted a dinner at Spaso House in honor of the Soviet leader at which time both Gorbachev and Reagan reviewed Soviet-American relations in a very positive manner. Lesser functional agreements were also signed; significant progress was recorded on the Angolan issue; but deadlock persisted on strategic arms reduction.

On the fourth day of the meeting, Gorbachev and Reagan formally exchanged the INF instruments of ratification, and in remarks on this occasion the General Secretary proclaimed this act to be a first major step in achieving his goal of a nuclear-free world, while the President described this superpower achievement a victory for "candor and realism." The Joint Statement issued on this fourth day discreetly and objectively summed up what was achieved and what was deferred at this summit meeting, following in the order of the established agenda. Subsequently, both leaders held separate press conferences during which they placed their own construction on the summit's failures and successes: Gorbachev judging it to be a "major event," but sharply criticizing the President and his aides in a series of complaints of "missed opportunities." At his press conference the President generally accented the positive with respect to the summit and put an optimistic gloss on the proceedings, a persistent line he followed in Moscow, even to noticeably supporting the General Secretary in his reform efforts. It was clear that the Soviets were disappointed in not achieving the success they expected on reducing strategic nuclear weapons by 50 percent.

On the final day, Thursday, June 2, the conference ended, and the President departed from Moscow for a brief stopover in London where he conferred with Prime Minister Thatcher and on the next day gave a major address at Guildhall where he reported on the proceedings in Moscow and voiced his general views on its meaning for East-West relations. He arrived in Washington on Friday, June 3, where in a welcoming ceremony he again reported on the achievements at Moscow in an address that was marked by an emotional and intensely patriotic affirmation of his own democratic philosophy.

RESULTS AND SIGNIFICANT ASPECTS
OF THE MOSCOW SUMMIT

Symbolism and ceremony plus some substantive achievements best describes the characteristics and results of the Moscow Summit. In general, the expectations on both sides were limited, and so were the results. Among the major achievements was the exchange of INF Treaty ratification instruments. Beyond that the practical achievements were modest, as for example in arms control: agreement on notification of missile testing. Agreements were also reached in such functional areas as international exchanges, space cooperation, maritime search and rescue, fisheries, transportation and radio navigation. An agreement in principle emerged in discussions on regional issues, specifically with respect to the withdrawal of Cuban troops from Angola, that in the long term proved to be very significant. The Soviet withdrawal from Afghanistan had a perceptible influence on its larger regional policy that conditioned the negotiating atmosphere.

Summit results can be measured against initial expectations, and judgments on success or failure made accordingly. But concrete results, such as in signing practical accords, are an incomplete criterion. For summitry is political interaction at the apex of national power. And it is often in this intangible area of inter-relationships where another and perhaps more accurate and realistic measure of success or failure can be taken. Both Gorbachev and Reagan recognized this when they passed their final judgments on the importance of the Moscow Summit. Both leaders acknowledged the limited achievements of the Moscow Summit, but the transcending significance for both was the conviction that their meeting had kept the superpower dialogue on track and moving forward. For Gorbachev, it was a "major event," a driving force in the "continuation of a dialogue." For Reagan, it represented a major step in the building of a "stable," "sustainable" and "long term" relationship. Uniformly both sides laid special stress on the high value of the meeting.

In sum, the Moscow Summit provided another unique opportunity for accelerating the momentum of what had become institutionalized Soviet-American summitry initiated in Geneva during November 1985. Moscow provided a forum for resolving differences through diplomacy and negotiations. It permitted political interaction at the highest level and accordingly opened up the possibility for inching ever so slowly forward in resolving major issues in dispute. Pomp and ceremony put a high gloss on this superpower dialogue, and largely only peripheral issues were eventually resolved. But serious business was, nonetheless, going on beneath it all. The deeper, unresolved issues in arms control that lay at the core-center of the relationship were addressed, but, ultimately, deferred for a future agenda.

As a negotiating encounter, the Moscow Summit is instructive for such activities as the pre-conference jockeying for position by the principals with special focus on attempts to shape the agenda and thus the outcome, Gorbachev making a strong pitch for arms control in the Washington Post interview and Reagan making an equally strong pitch for human rights in the various forums available to him. The conference also provides unique insights into the organization of such a vast diplomatic enterprise from the U.S. side, particularly the attempts to construct the proceedings and establish a schedule to best advance the President's own agenda preferences. For the Americans, the organization of the conference itself was a special challenge which seems to have been successfully met. The Soviets, operating with their own home-court advantage, had no comparable challenge.

Among other significant aspects of the summit was the role of the media, particularly the "open" media coverage in Moscow that seemed almost revolutionary. Though the President was given great visibility in the Soviet

Union, still his message was sometimes restricted and distorted. Nonetheless, the Moscow Summit marked further progress in Soviet handling (and manipulating) of the media. Unique also was the political role continuing to be played by the First Ladies which could establish a precedent for future summits. Finally, pomp and ceremony that seemed to be especially stressed at the Moscow Summit served the useful international purpose of highlighting conference diplomacy as a creative force in international relations. This fact alone may have strengthened the institutions and modalities of negotiations and diplomacy as instruments of peace and constituted a step forward towards creating a more peaceful and orderly world. In brief, the Moscow Summit symbolized another advance in the modern diplomatic tradition that has been evolving since the emergence of the nation-state in the late Middle Ages.

Both Gorbachev's and Reagan's negotiating performances were highly creditable. Both leaders had undertaken the essential tasks of diagnosing differences, formulating principles that from their own perspectives could constitute a basis for agreement, and conceptualizing a negotiating strategy. In carrying out their negotiating strategies both demonstrated great skill in pre-conference maneuvering, in attending to the externalities, and in bargaining at the negotiating table. Both revealed notable skills in negotiations, not only at the negotiating table itself but in the public forum.

Though the Moscow Summit was not a "turning point" in Soviet-American relations, it was the consummation of a development in the relationship that began at Geneva; it symbolized the transformation in the President's attitude towards the Soviet Union; and it reaffirmed and justified Gorbachev-Reagan policies that sought superpower accommodation. In brief, the Moscow Summit was a statement of faith in the value of diplomacy and negotiations.

No fifth Gorbachev-Reagan summit was held in the post-Moscow period as had been speculated. Differences over strategic arms control could not be resolved in the remaining months of the Reagan Administration; the task was passed on to the incoming Bush Administration.

This study was originally prepared for and published by the Congressional Research Service of the Library of Congress.

I believe that both of us have every reason to regard this meeting and your visit as a useful contribution to the development of dialogue between the Soviet Union and the United States....You and I have been dealing with each other for 3 years now. From the first exchange of letters to the conclusion of this meeting, we've come a long way. Our dialogue has not been easy, but we mustered enough realism and political will to overcome obstacles and divert the train of Soviet-U.S. relations from a dangerous track to a safer one.

—Gorbachev at departure ceremony
June 2, 1988

It is fitting that we are ending our visit, as we began it, in this hall named for the Order of St. George. I would like to think that our efforts during these past few days have slayed a few dragons and advanced the struggle against the evils that threaten mankind—threats to peace and to liberty. And I would like to hope that, like St. George, with God's help, peace and freedom can prevail.

—Reagan at departure ceremony
June 2, 1988

Introduction

In August 1988, the House Foreign Affairs Committee published a study prepared by Dr. Joseph G. Whelan, Senior Specialist in International Affairs of the Congressional Research Service entitled "Soviet Diplomacy and Negotiating Behavior, 1979–88: New Tests for U.S. Diplomacy."[1] The study concluded on the eve of the Moscow Summit meeting between General Secretary Mikhail Gorbachev and President Ronald Reagan scheduled for May 29–June 2, 1988. The current study, entitled "The Moscow Summit 1988: The Last Gorbachev-Reagan Negotiating Encounter," and also prepared by Dr. Whelan, examines this last major negotiation between both leaders, thus completing the coverage of Soviet diplomacy and negotiating behavior for the second Reagan Administration.

The study reviews pre-summit trends, the agenda, goals and expectations of both sides; surveys and analyzes the activities of each day from the eve of the opening of the summit until the President's departure from Moscow and arrival in Washington with a brief stopover in London; and analyzes the results and significant aspects of the meeting as a case study in Soviet-American negotiations. Sources on this summit meeting are limited to the official public record and media coverage on both sides since the main participants have yet to publish their personal memoirs that would provide the sort of insiders' accounts characteristic of volumes I and II of this series. Hence this is a macro-view of the Moscow Summit.

The author wishes to acknowledge with gratitude the assistance of the following staff of CRS who reviewed the study and offered constructive criticism: Dr. John P. Hardt, Senior Specialist in Soviet Economics; Francis T. Miko, Specialist in International Relations (Soviet Affairs); Dr. Stuart D. Goldman, Specialist in Soviet Affairs; and Jennifer Meade Schmidt, Review Office of CRS. Clerical support was provided by Linda S. Kline, Rita Banks and Ewen Allison.

I

Prelude to Moscow

A. PRE-SUMMIT TRENDS

1. Positive and Countervailing Forces

Two major trends dominated Soviet-American relations during the months prior to the Moscow Summit of mid-1988. The momentum of diplomatic accommodation continued along its upward swing, creating expectations of further progress in the coming superpower dialogue. But a countervailing trend persisted as both sides jockeyed for negotiating positions in pre-summit diplomacy, exacerbating the deeper, systemic discord that lay at the base of the relationship. Accordingly, the interaction of these competing forces produced a mood of positive expectation and promise as both sides prepared for the Moscow meeting, a mood mixed with a realistic belief that accomplishments would probably be more symbolic than substantive.

2. Elements of Accommodation: A New Era of Diplomacy and Negotiations

Planners for the Moscow Summit had a solid base upon which to construct this conference. Superpower relations had come a long way since the dark ages of September 1983 when in the aftermath of the Korean airliner shootdown relations had plummeted to a low reminiscent of the Cold War. Building on the positive turnaround initiated by Chernenko in 1984 and encouraged by the favorable reception of the Reagan Administration, General Secretary Gorbachev accelerated the pace of accommodation. Major benchmarks of this improving relationship were his meetings with President Reagan at Geneva in 1985, Reykjavik in 1986 and Washington in 1987.

These three summits, along with multiple conferences at the ministerial level, succeeded in reconstituting the superpower dialogue and in rebuild-

ST. PHILIP'S COLLEGE LIBRARY

ing the diplomatic framework of the relationship. Initiatives by both sides were gradually translated into concrete agreements. A high point, the penultimate, was reached with the signing of the INF Treaty at the Washington Summit in December 1987 and agreement to intensify negotiations on the gravest problem in the relationship and ultimate goal, the reduction of long-range strategic weapons by 50 percent. Other issues long in contention on the superpower agenda—regional problems, bilateral issues and human rights—were being managed with some satisfaction for both sides. Perhaps the tone and substance of this improving relationship was best expressed in the joint statement adopted at the conclusion of the Washington Summit which said in part:

> The two leaders recognized the special responsibility of the Soviet Union and the United States to search for realistic ways *to prevent confrontation and to promote a more sustainable and stable relationship* between their countries. To this end, they agreed to intensify dialogue and to encourage emerging trends towards constructive cooperation in all areas of their relations.[2]

Superpower relations had clearly entered a new era of diplomacy and negotiations by the eve of the Moscow Summit.[3] By this time both sides had actually achieved many of their objectives. The INF Treaty had addressed mutual concerns arising from the deployment of intermediate range missiles in Europe (the SS20's and Pershing II's) and accordingly eased pressures in that quarter. Renewed attention was now focused more intensely on a concern vital to both sides, the reduction of long-range strategic weapons. Pressures on regional issues abated somewhat with the Soviet decision to withdraw their troops from Afghanistan and with movement towards resolving the Angolan issue. The United States received some satisfaction on the human rights issue with the release of Andrei Sakharov, the granting of permission of dissidents and so-called refuseniks to emigrate, and the gradual easing of restrictions on freedom of expression internally under Gorbachev's policy of glasnost and perestroika.

In brief, much had been already accomplished by both sides, suggesting to some observers that Moscow might prove to be a "quiet summit."[4]

3.   Elements of Discord

a.   Failure in START Negotiations

Countervailing elements of discord in the relationship persisted, nonetheless, injecting some uncertainty as to the outcome at Moscow. Presummit contention centered on three major points: failure of the negotiators in

Geneva and Washington to resolve disagreements over long-range strategic missiles; Gorbachev's published resentment of Reagan's criticism of Soviet human rights violations and intervention in the Third World; and Soviet objections to certain individuals and groups to be present at the President's planned meetings with Soviet dissidents and during his visit to the Danilov Monastery.

On March 23, President Reagan announced that he would visit Moscow during May 29–June 2 for his fourth meeting with Gorbachev, the first visit of an American President to Moscow in 14 years. However, after two days of intensive negotiations in Washington between Soviet Foreign Minister Eduard A. Shevardnadze and Secretary of State George P. Shultz preceding the summit announcement, it seemed far from certain that a treaty reducing long-range strategic nuclear weapons would be reached in time for signature by the two leaders at Moscow.

Success of the INF Treaty, then in the ratification process, and the deadline for the Moscow Summit applied pressure on the negotiators in Geneva and the leaders in Moscow and Washington to wrap up the START negotiations. But agreement was blocked by failure to resolve a number of key issues including: interpretation of the ABM Treaty and agreements on future research, testing, development, and deployment of space-based ballistic missile defenses; limits on mobile ICBMs; limits on submarine-launched cruise missiles (SLCMs); and verification provisions.[5] In a realistic appraisal mixed with some optimism, Shevardnadze said after conferring with the President on March 22, with respect to meeting the summit deadline: "It is not an easy task. It is very complicated. There are many problems of a technical nature, but in principle it can be done. We are convinced it is possible."[6]

Failure to resolve these remaining control issues, therefore, contributed in no small measure to the build-up of discord.

b. Gorbachev's Complaints of Reagan's Criticism of Human Rights Violations and Third World Intervention

Gorbachev's public statements taking issue with President Reagan's criticism of Soviet human rights violations and Third World intervention added measurably to the pre-summit discord. But it must be kept in mind that Reagan's attacks and Gorbachev's counterattacks along with positive actions by both were part of the pre-summit diplomatic choreography intended to seek negotiating advantages and, therefore, deserve only passing reference as a "normal" tactical ploy in Soviet-American negotiations.

In three speeches in April, President Reagan pointedly criticized Soviet curtailment of freedom of expression in the Soviet Union and Soviet intervention, and thus attempted denial of democratic rights, in such Third World countries as Angola, Ethiopia, Nicaragua and Afghanistan. Accordingly, the President cautioned in one sweeping generalization that given these violations of human rights the West could "never have truly normal relations" with the Soviet Union.[7]

The Soviets, indeed, Gorbachev himself, took sharp exception to the President's remarks and in a meeting with Secretary Shultz on April 22 in Moscow, according to a Tass announcement, scolded Reagan for indulging in "obsolete stereotypes and at times malicious attacks against the Soviet Union." Gorbachev called the President's tone "confrontational" and added:

> We have so far been showing restraint, but if we reciprocate — and we can do so over a very wide range of issues — the atmosphere in Soviet-American relations can become such that it will make it no longer possible to solve any further issues.[8]

The Administration responded on April 25, through its spokesman Marlin Fitzwater, with a charge that the Soviets made "needlessly inflammatory" attacks on the President for his critical appraisal of Soviet policy. Despite the exchange one official said, seemingly with some truth, that the war of words was "less a flap than meets the eye," comparing it to the sharp exchanges prior to previous summit meetings. Secretary Shultz believed that Gorbachev had "overreacted" and that the whole affair was overblown.[9]

Presumably, the President took Gorbachev's criticism to heart; for in a speech on May 4, described as "unusually conciliatory," he praised the Soviet Union's recent human rights record and, in what was said to be a "rare acknowledgement," cited U.S. failings in such areas as homelessness and racial injustice.[10]

c.   Soviet Objections to Meetings with Dissidents

The Soviets were not happy about the President's scheduled meetings with dissidents and with one religious group at the Danilov Monastery. This proved to be another point of friction. Deputy Foreign Minister Vladimir F. Petrovsky, the official spokesman for the Soviet Foreign Ministry, set the tone of Soviet resentment when he said in a press conference, with a touch of sarcasm, that the Soviet side expected unofficial American meetings to include "broad circles of the Soviet public," but a meeting with dissidents "is hardly at improving mutual understanding."[11]

Soviet sensitivity on this issue was underscored when security officials in Leningrad reportedly warned two advocates of Jewish rights, both invited to meet with the President, that they should not attempt to make that meeting. Roald Zelichonok, one of the dissidents, said he was told that unspecified "administrative measures" would be taken if he disregarded the warning. Another dissident, Yevgeny Lein, was also warned to stay away or, like his co-religionist, would "live to regret it if they went to the Reagan meeting."[12]

When reports of the threats reached Helsinki where the President was resting to recover from jet lag prior to his departure on the final leg of his journey to Moscow, White House officials held consultations with Soviet authorities. According to one aide, "we have assurances that everyone invited will be allowed to attend."[13]

Similarly, the Soviets objected to one of the religious groups scheduled to meet with the President in a separate session at the Danilov Monastery near Moscow. Again, after further discussions with Soviet authorities, the problem was resolved and the meeting was allowed to take place as scheduled.[14]

4. Positive Expectations Tempered by Realism

The road to the Moscow Summit was, therefore, hardly a smooth one. The interaction of positive and negative forces noted above produced a mood of hopeful expectation and promise mixed with a realistic assessment that accomplishments would probably be more symbolic than substantive.

But the overarching reality was clear; namely, that both Gorbachev and Reagan wanted the summit to succeed, for reasons that will be specifically elaborated below. Continuation of the superpower dialogue at the highest level was for both a prime political interest. Contention in the months prior to Moscow suggests a normal negotiating tactic as both sides attempted, among other tactical goals, to influence the agenda, hoping to affect the outcome of the summit to their advantage.

What is most significant, however, is that the meeting was taking place and that further momentum was gathering in support of a political dialogue that had begun in Geneva during November 1985. So anxious was the President for success at Moscow that when failure to reach agreement on strategic arms became clear on the eve of the meeting, he raised the possibility of a fifth meeting with Gorbachev, perhaps in "a neutral locale," if a treaty was not ready for signing before he left office in January 1989.[15] Gorbachev, who was to face a major test of his leadership at the politically crucial 19th Party Conference in late June, was equally anxious for success at the summit.

B. AGENDA FOR THE MOSCOW MEETING

1. Pre-Summit Perspectives

Americans approached the Moscow Summit with limited expectations. Hopes for the signing of a long-range strategic nuclear weapons agreement, the expected centerpiece of the summit, never great among some observers, faded rapidly as the negotiators failed to resolve their differences in last minute efforts, though some officials seemed to hope (perhaps against hope) that some progress, if not a breakthrough, could be achieved.[16] As Maj. Gen. William F. Burns, the new director of the Arms Control and Disarmament Agency, remarked pessimistically in response to an inquiry as to whether he thought new proposals would be advanced in Moscow, "I don't see any tremendous breakthrough on either side."[17]

This unpromising forecast seemed based on the fact that no major changes were produced in the U.S. positions after a series of pre-summit White House meetings, nor were there positive signs from the Soviet side. Burns expressed the prevailing view within the Administration that to complete a START treaty in 1988 would be a "daunting" task. Even the INF treaty was encountering some unexpected snags in the Senate ratification process: Chief of Staff Howard H. Baker, Jr. predicted that it "will be a tight squeeze to see if the Senate does complete action on that before the President reaches Moscow."[18]

Thus, the U.S. side had only modest expectations that the Moscow Summit would produce any substantive achievements, and, accordingly, Administration officials tended to downplay its prospects. "We've asked ourselves how best to describe what this is and is not," said Ms. Rozanne Ridgway, Assistant Secretary of State for European Affairs, "and we all agree it is not a high watermark."[19] President Reagan's meetings with the General Secretary (five were scheduled) were thus expected to be heavy on symbolism and ceremony.[20] Some Administration officials acknowledged that the summit would be a television spectacular, revolving around the President's public appearances.[21] Yet, with respect to issues to be discussed, Marlin Fitzwater said that the summit would not focus only on arms control but rather on four or five issues "across-the-board" in Soviet-American relations.[22]

In contrast to U.S. expressions of limited expectations (at most seeing the value of the upcoming summit only in extending the pattern of regular top-level superpower contacts), the Soviets were seen as more hopeful. They agreed that regular contacts were important. But they were looking for movement on a number of key issues, notably the speeding up of the START negotiations and the opening of negotiations on conventional arms. For the Soviets, arms control was their primary interest. As one observer remarked, "As so often in the past, Moscow appears to believe that everything will flow from arms control."[23]

Thus, Soviet-American pre-summit perspectives were asymmetrical: The Americans foresaw a meeting marked by symbolism and ceremony; the Soviets looked for positive movement on their arms control agenda.

2. Arms Control

By the time of the Moscow meeting, the overall agenda for Gorbachev-Reagan summit conferences, pressed by the United States and now accepted by the Soviets as a four-part agenda, had taken on a fairly routine pattern; namely, arms control, regional issues, human rights and humanitarian issues, and problems in bilateral relations. Arms control, the vital center of the concentric circles of the relationship, had top priority.[24]

The Moscow Summit appeared to offer the superpowers the possibility of reviving prospects for completing a new START agreement before the President left office. Negotiations in Geneva had stalled over serious disagreements, putting pressure, therefore, on the conferees at Moscow. As one observer explained, "In recent months, the steam has gone out of the arms negotiations in Geneva, and the heady talk of completing a pact before the end of the year has been replaced by a grudging recognition of the difficulties that lie ahead."[25]

These difficulties can be summed up simply as the inability of the negotiators to resolve such key issues as the interpretation of the ABM Treaty and agreements on future research, testing, development and deployment of space-based ballistic missile defenses – in brief, SDI; limits on mobile ICBMs; limits on submarine-launched cruise missiles (SLCMs); and verification provisions.[26]

These disputed issues were expected to be aired at Moscow along with other arms control problems, but differences between the sides had thus far proved to be fundamental and irreconcilable. For example, the Soviets opposed SDI and sought to restrict its development by insisting on a strict interpretation of the ABM Treaty that would limit testing and thus its development. In contrast, the United States refused to budge on SDI and insisted on a broader interpretation that permits testing and thus further development. Differences over the SLCMs were similarly fundamental, the U.S. side opposing limitations because compliance could not be adequately verified, the Soviets insisting that verifiable limits should be set.[27]

Prior to the Moscow Summit there were no signs on the horizon to encourage the belief that the broad area of disagreement over the many esoteric technical issues in strategic nuclear arms would be narrowed. In an interview with Washington Post correspondents on the eve of the conference, Gorbachev said it would be "senseless" not to limit space weapons or sea-launched cruise missiles in an arms treaty being negotiated at Geneva. Yet he expressed hope. "We see genuine possibilities to resolve all of these questions...together and to have a treaty on a 50 percent reduction of strategic offensive arms," Gorbachev said.[28]

But Soviet inflexibility, U.S. failure to develop a consensus within the Administration on the many highly technical issues in arms control and the complexity of the issues, gave credence to General Burns' pessimistic forecast that it would be "extremely difficult" to achieve agreement by the end of the Reagan Administration, though he acknowledged that, "There is always the possibility that something will happen."[29]

Arms control was, therefore, expected to be given a full airing at the Moscow Summit, but agreement, at least on the central areas of conflict in strategic nuclear weapons, was not realistically expected. On the other hand, progress in other areas of arms control could offset any disappointment in the strategic nuclear arms area. The Soviets were eager for a final ceremonial exchange of the ratified INF Treaty. Verification procedures called for in that treaty could help, in the Soviet view, break deadlocks in other arms control areas, including chemical weapons and conventional weapons.[30] Exchange of ratifications was put firmly on the agenda when on May 28, at the time of the President's departure from Helsinki to Moscow, the Senate approved the treaty by a vote of 93-5.[31]

Less formidable agreements in the arms control area were expected to be reached at Moscow, such as: one requiring both sides to give each other notice of any nuclear missile tests; one spelling out verification procedures for peaceful nuclear explosions; and a third that would codify procedures for carrying out experiments at nuclear test sites.[32]

3.   Regional Problems

Since adopting a policy of globalism in the mid-1950's, the Soviet Union expanded its activities throughout the Third World where this sometimes aggressive and provocative policy often collided with U.S. and Western interests. Serious students of the Third World have long been concerned about the great potential for East-West confrontation in the various regional "hot spots," as they were called. For this reason, and the desire to check Soviet expansionism, the United States has insisted that regional problems be listed prominently on any summit agenda.

However, under Gorbachev, Soviet policy in the Third World was changing, in some cases, radically. Indeed, evidence was accumulating of a Soviet effort to retrench in parts of the Third World where it was over-committed. A decision had been made and agreement reached on Soviet military withdrawal from Afghanistan. Change in Soviet policy towards Cambodia seemed in the offing. Relations with China were improving, signalling a changed view in the Asian-Pacific region. Progress was apparent in the Angolan issue that would entail the withdrawal of Cuban troops. And there was evidence that Soviet involvement in Nicaragua was stabilizing.[33] Both sides called for cooperation on resolving regional issues, but substantial disagreements and mutual suspicion remained, nonetheless, notably in the Middle East and Persian Gulf.[34]

Regional issues were, therefore, expected to play, and did play, an important role in the Moscow Summit. (The two countries agreed to a joint position on objectives and a time-frame for withdrawal from Angola. Subsequent events in Angola showed that this was a breakthrough to eventual agreement.) The United States was expected to encourage continued Soviet withdrawal from Afghanistan and disengagement from Angola. As Ridgway said, "It seems that perhaps southern Africa is the regional issue that offers some prospect for moving...the dialogue ahead."[35] Other regions expected to get the attention of the summit negotiators were the Middle East and the Persian Gulf where the Iran-Iraq war continued; the Korean Peninsula, Cambodia, Central America and Ethiopia where uncertainty and discord prevailed.[36]

4. Human Rights and Humanitarian Issues

Human rights and humanitarian issues (as the Soviets prefer) have long been troublesome matters in Soviet-American relations. Systemic and ideological differences were the root cause. Over the years the United States had taken its measure of Soviet good conduct in international relations in part by their performance in respecting the human rights of their people and others with whom they were dealing. U.S. attention generally focused on specific Soviet policy towards political dissent, religious practice, rights of ethnic and national minorities, and the right of emigration. Sensitive to their own Communist values, preferences and political practices, the Soviet leadership resented what they termed U.S. intervention in internal Soviet affairs. Still, the Americans held fast to their position over the years and insisted, as in past summits, that human rights be a priority item on the agenda, much to the chagrin of the Soviets.

Under Gorbachev, internal repression had been eased and respect for human rights of Soviet citizens improved. In February 1986, for example, Anatoly Shchransky, a prominent Jewish dissident in the pre-Gorbachev years, was released from prison and permitted to emigrate to Israel. In December, Andrei Sakharov's internal exile in Gorki was ended, and he was permitted to return to Moscow. In January 1987, more than 100 political prisoners, including prominent dissidents, were released from prison. Jewish emigration was also liberalized. In 1987, the number of Jewish emigrants increased to 8,155, including many long-term refuseniks, the highest total since 1981. Between January to November 1988, the total rose to over 15,000.[37] The trend of improvement, notably in freedom of expression, also continued.

President Reagan acknowledged Soviet progress in human rights, even to the point of admitting American infractions. But he, nonetheless, was determined to continue pressing his case in Moscow. He did this in three ways: by calling attention to the human rights problem in pre-summit maneuvering, as in his speech at Helsinki honoring the Final Act of 1975, a basic international charter on human rights; by making sure that the issue was high on the formal summit agenda; and finally by calling attention to American concerns in a practical and tangible way by meeting with dissidents and religious figures and by mixing with the general public, conveying thereby explicitly and by indirection this concern for continued improvement in the exercise of their rights.

For this reason U.S. planners scheduled specific meetings with dissidents, religious figures and Soviet intellectuals, and provided for informal forays among the people, as Gorbachev had done during the Washington Summit. Fitzwater explained that the meeting at the Danilov Monastery was intended "to symbolize our concern for religious freedom."[38] The Gorbachev-Reagan one-on-one talks will be important, he said, "but the outside meetings will be as important. They will show the U.S. position symbolically, and they are closely tied to the President's meetings."[39] Noting the President's desire for personal contacts with Soviet citizens, another senior Administration official remarked, "I think it's symbolic, but it's also the President's genuine desire...really to listen to people, to hear their concerns, and to learn."[40]

5.   Bilateral Issues

Bilateral issues, a catch-all for all other problems in Soviet-American relations, mostly functional, was the last category on the agenda for the Moscow Summit. Ridgway noted that a number of agreements were nearing completion in the maritime area, including ones covering search and rescue procedures, ocean pollution, transportation technologies and fishing rights. A three-year cultural agreement and an agreement on cooperation in basic scientific research could also be approved.[41] Trade in non-strategic goods was also expected to be discussed.[42]

C.   GORBACHEV'S EXPECTATIONS AND GOALS

1.   The Washington Post Interview, May 22, 1988

Negotiators preparing for a major encounter with an adversary generally engage in a good deal of pre-conference maneuvering. The purpose is to seek whatever advantages are possible by intimidating the other side (a favorite Khrushchev ploy), by scoring points through skewing or prioritizing the agenda (always a stock-in-trade Soviet maneuver), by setting forth expectations and goals in anticipation of success as a way of adding pressure to the other side (a Gorbachev tactic employed many times), and, in general, by creating a favorable negotiating atmosphere sympathetic to the interests of one side and detrimental to the other. Both Gorbachev and Reagan engaged in such maneuvering immediately before the Moscow meeting.

Prominent among Gorbachev's efforts to influence the upcoming summit was an extended interview with The Washington Post's chairman and senior editors that was published in extenso on May 22, 1988.[43] The interview was 90 minutes long; it contained responses to specific questions presented in advance; and these responses were expanded upon in a face-to-face interview with Gorbachev. The entire coverage consumed four printed pages of The Post.

Briefly, in the interview Gorbachev reviewed his internal reform policy identified generally as perestroika and glasnost and restated his commitment to "new thinking" in Soviet foreign policy, a Gorbachev formulation calling for the restructuring of foreign policy to conform to the policies and goals of internal reform. Implicitly and explicitly, his remarks were intended to show the inter-relationship between both and convey an appealing positive impression of Soviet policy for global consumption. Gorbachev made the following points that had a direct bearing on his negotiating position at the upcoming Moscow Summit.

The State of the Cold War: I am convinced that positive trends are unfolding in the world. There is a turn from confrontation to coexistence. The winds of the Cold War are being replaced by the winds of hope. And I see that a significant role in that process is being played by the signs of improvement in the relations between the United States and the Soviet Union. All over the world there is an acute need for change or, if you wish, a need for restructuring international relations. In that situation it is essential to continue positive contacts between the East and the West.[44]

On Continuing Soviet-American Dialogue: As for the dialogue between the United States and the Soviet Union, it is simply vital because of the great role they play in today's world.

The very fact of that dialogue is working for peace, not to mention its content with such exceptionally important joint statements as those regarding the inadmissibility of wars, nuclear or any other, the necessity of resolving problems by political means and of recognizing the realities of today's world.

It is very important that all this has sounded loud and clear for the whole world to hear, and we have seen how the world has responded to it. All this leads to the following conclusion: Yes, we are all different and remain so. We will remain loyal to our ideas and our way of life. But we have a common responsibility, especially our two great powers, and our every action must measure up to that responsibility.[45]

* * *

The experience of present-day international relations shows the paramount importance of meetings between leaders of states, all the more so when the case in point is the United States and the Soviet Union. Since both countries are well aware of the need for intensifying the dialogue and improving relations, it is absolutely obvious that it is not only the leaders' personal views that matter. This is the imperative of our time. This is the striving of our peoples. Such is the constant in the Soviet-American dialogue. It remains intact. And if we add to that the experience we have accumulated, all these factors taken together give rise to hopes for continuity and even for intensified contacts and improved mutual understanding. However, let me repeat that everything rests on the interests of our countries and peoples, not on the sentiments of individual political figures or their personal motives. No one can allow relations to slide to a point beyond which the unpredictable may happen. Such is the basis for continuing and developing the Soviet-American dialogue. It will remain the same in the future as well.

In a word, we are interested in developing the dialogue, we will strive to make it more productive, we will try to facilitate the "adaptation" of the next U.S. administration to contacts with us, and will do everything within our power to keep the process begun in Geneva in 1985 from stopping. And, naturally enough, we hope for the same attitude on the American side.[46]

Appraisal of Reagan and Confidence in Reaching Agreement: I'm not particularly fond of giving personal character references. But since you ask, I would like to say that realism is an important quality in President Reagan as a politician. By this I mean the ability to adapt one's views to the changing situations, while remaining faithful to one's convictions.[47]

Confidence in Creating a Nuclear-Free World: I cannot agree with those who think the drive for a nuclear-free world is hopeless.

I have argued more than once with representatives of the West over their case that without nuclear weapons we would never have survived for 40 years without another world war. This is just a conjecture. But what about a sober evaluation of the real role played by the so-called "balance of fear?" It has given us nothing but unheard of militarization of foreign policies, economies and even intellectual life. It has caused damage in the sphere of international morality and ethics and has killed the atmosphere of mutual trust, friendliness and sincere interest in each other which was born in Soviet-American relations in the years of joint warfare and victory over fascism.

I am convinced that strategic military parity can be maintained at a low level and without nuclear weapons. We have clearly formulated our choice: to stop, then reverse the arms race....

A peaceful future for mankind can be guaranteed not by "nuclear deterrence," but by a balance of reason and good will and by a system of comprehensive security.[48]

On Positive Results in Strategic Offensive Weapons Discussions: As for the potential results of the upcoming fourth meeting with the president and, notably, the prospects for a detailed agreement on a 50 percent cut in strategic offensive weapons, the past few months and weeks have seen so much speculation that I would like to make the following point: Be patient, the meeting is just a few days away, let the president and I work together. Whatever we arrive at will certainly not be concealed from the public.

There are two more points to be made here, though. The very continuation of the Soviet-American dialogue at the summit level is important and substantive. In any case, I hope our attention will be focused on the main international problems, like at the previous meetings, and that we will be able to rise to a new level of dialogue and mutual understanding.

And next, if an agreement on a 50 percent reduction in strategic offensive weapons comes to be drafted under the present U.S. administration, I see no reason why President Reagan and I should not sign it. I would certainly welcome that.[49]

Favoring a Strict Construction of the ABM Treaty: I believe that which is contained in the statement on the understanding of the ABM [Anti-Ballistic Missile] treaty in the form that was accepted in 1972 and as we understood it until 1983 — that does provide a basis to move forward toward 50 percent reductions in strategic offensive arms. But only in that way, in no other.[50]

Opposition to SDI: But I think you would agree with me that if I say that if we sign with one hand a treaty reducing strategic offensive forces in one area and at the same time launch an arms race in space or at sea, what would be the point? That would be senseless.

And so this is not capricious, it isn't some kind of maneuver from the Soviet side, but rather a carefully thought-out and responsible position. I think it is in the interest of the Soviet people, of the American people and the people of the world. If we just replace one kind of arms race with another, particularly in space, where the arms race would take a particularly dramatic turn, we would undermine the trust that has begun to be built, we would make worthless all the experience that we have accumulated at the Geneva negotiations. This new kind of arms race, new sphere for an arms race, new criteria — it would take decades to reach some kind of agreement....

I think that he who pushes for an arms race in space is committing a crime against the people — his own people, and others. That must be said with all responsibility, and with clarity. Such an approach, such an idea, is a road to destabilization, to unpredictability on matters of security. This must be condemned, the initiator of such an approach must be pilloried.[51]

Resolution of Regional Problems: Yes, it [the Soviet Union] is prepared [to cooperate with the United States and other countries in resolving other conflicts besides Afghanistan, for example in Central America, the Persian Gulf and Angola]. I have already said that, given constructive cooperation between the Soviet Union and the United States and major emphasis on the prestige and capabilities of the United Nations, its Security Council and other bodies, political settlement of regional conflicts and prevention of new ones will gradually become an international practice, a norm. I would like to confirm this conviction of mine.

The world has ample proof that dragged-out conflicts are the results of politics being exposed to pressure from outdated stereotypes. They are orthodox approaches to national security, with power politics being preferred to sober considerations and political boldness, the old habit of seeking to satisfy one's rights and interests at other people's expense, and a shortage of fairness and humaneness in international relations.

The president and I have discussed this more than once and we will have a chance to take up these matters at the forthcoming meeting, too. Of course, such talk can be productive only if there is respect for the right of every people to choose their own road.[52]

On Human Rights as a Problem: Our perestroika, the main factor of which is creative effort, also includes doing away with all deformation of the past years, with everything that hampers manifestation of the humanitarian essence of socialism.

We know our problems and speak honestly and openly about them. The process of democratization does not bypass the sphere of human rights and liberties. We are enhancing the political and public status of the human personality. Many issues have already been resolved within the framework of the democratic process, while others will be resolved as Soviet society changes qualitatively in the course of perestroika. But that is our job. We are resolving these issues not because we want to play up to somebody or to please somebody, but because this meets the interests of our society, because perestroika cannot be carried on without it, and, last but not least, because it is wanted by the Soviet people who have long outgrown the restrictions which they put up with in the past and which were to a certain extent an inevitable part of the unusual revolutionary development which we have gone through.

Once I said...: Please, show me a country that has no problems. Each country has problems of its own, human rights included. Of course, we are well-informed about the situation with political, social, economic and other rights in the United States. We know well the achievements and problems, but also the flaws of American society. But we do not tolerate interference in your home affairs, though we deem it right to express our views on the processes taking place in American society, on your administration's policy. But we do not want to make all this a reason for confrontation....I want to emphasize once again that we do not try to impose anything on the United States, but at the same time we rebuff attempts by any side to meddle in our affairs, no matter who tries to do so in your country....For the sake of our mutual understanding, please, do not try to teach us to live according to American rules — it is altogether useless.[53]

2. Significance of the Gorbachev Interview for Negotiations at Moscow

Various meanings can be seen in Gorbachev's interview that bear on the expected outcome of the Moscow Summit and reflect Gorbachev's appraisal of Soviet-American relations at that time. Gorbachev endorses the popular belief in the de-compression of the Cold War. He restates his faith in a continuing (and necessary) dialogue with the United States, and restates his faith also in President Reagan as a realistic negotiating partner with whom agreements can be reached and thus mutual interests achieved. He does not doubt that his goal of a nuclear-free world can be accomplished and, accordingly, invests in the negotiations on strategic offensive weapons a positive and appealing content.

Still, he lays down anew his opposition to SDI and voices again his opposition to efforts to advance a loose-construction of the ABM Treaty that justifies its further development. To the General Secretary, withdrawal from Afghanistan is an "earnest" of the Soviet intention to resolve regional problems peacefully. But on human rights he cites internal Soviet progress under perestroika thus far but emphasizes both the limits and the innate irreconcilability of Soviet and American views on this matter.

In brief, Gorbachev's is an affirmative statement of Soviet negotiating positions as he enters the summit meeting. But it is also a re-statement of his commitment to dialogue and negotiations – "a juggling act," as one Post reporter termed it. More than that, it is a realistic restatement of Soviet views apparently designed to appeal to a world hoping for peace between the superpowers with the expectation of gaining some support for the Soviet side. To this extent, it constitutes a formidable statement, sweeping in scope and penetrating in depth, not only of Soviet expectations and goals as they enter negotiations in Moscow, but also as a strong counter-pressure on the U.S. negotiators.

D.   REAGAN'S EXPECTATIONS AND GOALS

1.   To Advance the Cause of Peace and Human Freedom

In a series of statements, speeches and an interview by Soviet journalists to be aired over Soviet television, President Reagan set forth his own expectations and goals to be achieved at Moscow. Perhaps none better summed up his thinking than his departure statement at the White House on May 25, when he recalled his remarks upon leaving for the Geneva Summit in 1985:

> I told you that my mission, simply stated was a mission for freedom and peace. I wanted to sit down across the table from Mr. Gorbachev and try to set out with him a basis for peaceful discourse and cooperation between our two countries, at the same time working to advance the cause and frontiers of human freedom.

The President recalled that he wanted to "establish a better working relationship with the Soviet Union – one no longer subject to the dangerous highs and lows of the past." A working relationship, he explained, that "would be based on realities, not merely on a seeming relaxation of tensions" between the two superpowers "that could quickly disappear." To accomplish this goal he believed that "solid and steady progress" had to be made in areas important for U.S. interests: human rights, regional conflicts, arms reductions and bilateral exchanges—in that order.

"We've come a long way since then," the President continued, and he proceeded to enumerate the areas of achievements in Soviet-American relations since Geneva, such as, agreement on the Soviet withdrawal from Afghanistan; agreement reached on intermediate range missiles; progress in reducing strategic offensive weapons by 50 percent; improvements in Soviet human rights; and expanded bilateral exchanges.

Impressive as these achievements were, the President observed, "they represent only a beginning." In his meeting with Gorbachev in Moscow, the President acknowledged that, "we will be looking to the future, for there remains much to be done." And then he proceeded to explain his priorities and goals in a four-part agenda:

On Human Rights: I will press to see that the positive trends I've mentioned continue and the reforms are made permanent. We certainly welcome the recent signs of Soviet progress toward greater freedom of religion, greater freedom of speech, greater freedom of movement. There have been indications that this progress may be written into Soviet law and regulations so that it can be a more permanent part of Soviet life. We will be doing all we can to encourage just that.

Concerning Regional Conflicts: We'll be looking for Soviet actions to help advance negotiations on the Angola and Namibia problems and to support UN efforts to end the Iran-Iraq war. We will ask the Soviets to use their influence with the Ethiopian Government to prevent a manmade crisis of starvation there. We'll urge the Soviets to help move the Middle East peace process closer to a just and lasting solution. And we'll look for ways to help the parties resolve other regional conflicts in Africa, Asia, and, yes, Central America.

Regarding Arms Reductions: We'll strive to resolve the issues that still stand in the way of our agreement to cut U.S. and Soviet strategic offensive nuclear arms in half. As we make progress, our negotiators will be able to move forward in their work on the draft START [strategic arms reduction talks] treaty. We'll continue to seek ways to improve the verification procedures of two existing treaties on nuclear testing—the Peaceful Nuclear Explosions Treaty and the Threshold Test Ban Treaty—so that those treaties can be ratified. And I will urge the Soviets to move ahead at the Vienna follow-up meeting of the Conference on Security and Cooperation in Europe. At these discussions, negotiators from 35 nations are working on ways to advance human rights and strengthen the confidence- and security-building measures they negotiated at Stockholm in 1986. Separately, the 23 members of the Atlantic Alliance and Warsaw Pact are negotiating a mandate for new talks on conventional forces. Success here means the Soviets must make continued progress on human rights, for the security in Europe involves much more than military arrangements. It must be based on a solid foundation of respect for the rights of individuals.

Concerning Bilateral Relations: We will address both new agreements and renewals of existing agreements to extend the areas in which we cooperate. This will include everything from practical matters of nuclear safety to radio-navigation and the protection of our global environment. We'll seek to broaden still further our people-to-people contacts and, especially, to give more of our young people the opportunity to participate in such exchanges.[54]

2.   Significance of Reagan's Views for the Moscow Meeting

For President Reagan the main issue at Moscow was to be human rights. He made this point in virtually all of his major utterances, particularly in his departure statement where he placed human rights as number one on the agenda and in his formal address in Finlandia Hall in Helsinki where he commemorated the 13th anniversary of the signing of the Helsinki Final Act.[55] The central theme in the Helsinki Final Act was recognition of human rights as a key principle in improving East-West relations.

For the President human rights was the first item on the Moscow agenda for two reasons. In his view the fulfillment of human rights and the achievement of security were indissolubly linked. Human freedom was a primary condition for peace and security. As he said in Helsinki, "security and human rights must be advanced together or cannot truly be secured at all."[56] In a radio address at Helsinki he expanded on this theme:

History has taught us that it is not weapons that cause war but the nature and conduct of governments that wield the weapons. So, when we encourage Soviet reforms, it is with the knowledge that democracy not only guarantees human rights, but also helps prevent war, and, in truth, is a form of arms control. So, really, our whole agenda has one purpose: to protect peace, freedom, and life itself.[57]

Hence the necessity of advancing human rights at Moscow.

Secondly, differences in arms control negotiations, particularly on reducing strategic offensive weapons by 50 percent, were not likely to be narrowed at Moscow, though progress could possibly be sufficient to warrant a fifth summit before the President left office. Both leaders kept this door open. With limited expectations in arms control, therefore, White House planners placed great emphasis on human rights and human contacts, such highly visible events as meetings with Soviet intellectuals, religious leaders and university students, along with informal forays among the Soviet people (in the manner of Gorbachev during the Washington Summit). Taking full advantage of the President's strength as a person-to-person communicator, summit planners designed his itinerary along the lines of a political campaign swing with heavy emphasis on visual impressions and emotional impact that he was expected to generate. As Tom Griscom, the director of White House communications, noted, "We will be offering encouragement; we will be offering a willingness to help in the process of change."[58] In brief, the President would publicly acknowledge the progress already made in Soviet democratization under Gorbachev's reform policies and encourage its continued advance.

In his own way, therefore, Reagan was attempting to shape the agenda, influence the negotiations at Moscow and further U.S. interests as he perceived them.

E. "HIDDEN" AGENDAS

Gorbachev and Reagan also had their "hidden" agendas as they prepared to meet in Moscow. Each presumably hoped to use the summit as a prestige-producing event to fortify their own political positions at home. By the Spring of 1988, Gorbachev had made great progress towards consolidating his authority in Moscow, though he had a long way to go before establishing uncontestably Socialist legitimacy for his rule. He was facing a critical 19th Party Conference in late June at which time he was expected to push through fundamental changes in the structure of the Soviet Government. The conference was also expected to provide the platform for criticism of his reform policies by conservative opponents. He had hoped that the Moscow Summit would coincide more closely with the opening of the Party Conference, but without success. In the background of the summit proceedings, therefore, there was believed to be this unstated expectation that the summit would strengthen Gorbachev's internal political position, enabling him to proceed with his structural reforms of the Soviet system.[59]

The same can be said for Reagan. He, too, had his "hidden" agenda. Besides wanting to crown his presidency with the historic legacy of a major success at the summit, thus leaving a favorable mark for his Administration on history, it was reported that the President saw the summit as an opportunity for "refurbishing" his presidency. As the first U.S. President to visit Moscow in 14 years, Reagan's advisers reportedly looked forward to the Gorbachev meeting as an opportunity to refocus attention on Soviet-American affairs and divert it from the troubling and embarrassing issues that proved damaging to the presidency in the Spring of 1988. Among these embarrassments were the controversies over the Administration's Panama policy in its failed attempt to remove the dictator Noriega, the damaging influence of the North-Contra Aid affair, the purported conflicts of interests of Attorney General Edwin Meese III, a long-time Reagan friend and adviser, and the critical and unflattering portraits of the President in books published by several of his former aides.[60]

Both leaders, therefore, had good reason not only to meet in Moscow, but also to make their meeting a visible success.[61]

II

Summit Meeting in Moscow

A. FIRST DAY, SUNDAY, MAY 29

1. Prevailing Political Atmosphere and President's Arrival in Moscow

Upon leaving Helsinki for Moscow, President Reagan was fully prepared to advance his agenda in talks with the General Secretary and to pursue vigorously and imaginatively the public relations side of the visit as designed by his advisers. Yet, as he said at the time of his initial departure in Washington, "I don't expect it to be easy." He acknowledged that "many differences, deep differences, moral differences" divided both countries, but he voiced confidence, nonetheless, that these differences could be surmounted. "We're still fellow human beings," he noted. "We can still work together to keep the peace."[62]

The political atmosphere seemed to be one of hopeful expectation mixed with anticipation of modest achievement, especially in arms control. The Americans seemed to downplay any anticipated success in arms control, while placing greater stress on human rights and the ceremonial side of summitry. The Soviet media put a positive face on the meeting as an important advance in bilateral relations, while at the same time the Soviet leadership and prominent commentators sought to minimize expectations over possible accomplishments in Moscow, finally acknowledging that it was unlikely that any major arms control agreement would be concluded.[63]

In short, both sides tended to generate a political atmosphere of caution and restraint, suffused, nonetheless, with anticipation of a positive and successful meeting. It was within this generally favorable political atmosphere that Air Force One touched down at Vnukovo Airport, east of Moscow, at 2 p.m., Sunday, May 29. On this bright and warm spring day, a pleasant breeze rippled the Soviet and American flags flying over the airport. A streamer on the airport building read in Russian and English, "Welcome, Mr. President." All external signs seemed to augur well for the upcoming meeting with the General Secretary.

The large American delegation (estimated in all at 600) included: Secretary of State George P. Shultz; Secretary of Defense Frank C. Carlucci; White House Chief of Staff Howard H. Baker; White House national security adviser Lt. Gen. Colin L. Powell; and Max M. Kampelman, the chief arms control negotiator.

The President and Mrs. Reagan were greeted by a small group of Soviet officials headed by President Andrei A. Gromyko, Foreign Minister Eduard A. Shevardnadze, and Anatoly F. Dobrynin, former Soviet Ambassador to the United States until his appointment in 1986 as a leading official in the powerful and prestigious Secretariat in charge of foreign affairs.

After Mrs. Reagan was presented a large bouquet of red roses, Gromyko and the President walked to the Soviet honor guard lined up along the tarmac. As the national anthems of both countries were played, the commander presented the honor guard to the President, followed by an inspection of it by Gromyko and Reagan. Ceremonial protocol was meticulously followed for such occasions, protocol that has political meaning beyond the ritual.

A touch of authentic and "homey" Americanism was added to the proceedings when about 100 members of the U.S. Embassy staff and their families, including many children dressed casually in T-shirts and jeans, waved small American flags in greeting the Reagans as they walked hand-in-hand down the ramp of the plane. No ordinary Soviet citizens were allowed on the airport grounds, but military bands and drill teams performed for the President.

The formal and official ceremony of greeting completed, the President and his party left the airport in a motorcade for the 30-minute drive to the inner city where they were scheduled to receive a formal welcome by the General Secretary at the ornate St. George's Hall in the Kremlin. As the President's limousine entered the gates of this citadel of Soviet power, a Soviet television commentator quoted approvingly the words of an American newspaper article that said: "The fact that the American president is appearing in the Kremlin, the capital of what he once called the "evil empire," raises hope that the Cold War may by now be ending."[64]

2. Welcoming Ceremony at St. George's Hall

a. The Setting

The General Secretary greeted the Reagans in a welcoming ceremony at St. George's Hall in the Grand Kremlin Palace. They were met by Gorbachev and his wife, Raisa, in the center of the Hall where they exchanged handshakes and greetings. According to Pravda, the President was greeted "warmly" by the General Secretary. A pool of photographers, newsreel cameramen and television crews recorded the entire ceremony on film for transmission to many countries throughout the world.[65]

b. Gorbachev's Remarks

Speaking in Russian with consecutive translation into English, the General Secretary extended his "sincere greetings" to the President, noting that it was almost six months since the Washington Summit, which he termed a "major milestone" in the history of Soviet-American relations and international relations. The political dialogue was now to continue, he said, "a fact we duly appreciate." "Meaningful assessments" could already be made: "long-held dislikes have been weakened; habitual stereotypes stemming from enemy images have been shaken loose." As a result, the "human features of the other nation are now more clearly visible." According to Gorbachev, this change itself was important because "history has objectively bound our two countries by a common responsibility for the destinies of mankind." All peoples, particularly the Soviet and the American, welcomed the "emerging positive changes" in the relationship and hoped that this Moscow Summit "will be productive, providing a fresh impetus in all areas of dialogue and interaction" between the two nations.

Acknowledging that both leaders were conscious of the "longing for mutual understanding, cooperation, and a safe and stable world" among their peoples, Gorbachev reiterated his agenda, citing first the necessity of discussing "constructively the main aspects of disarmament"; namely, the issues relating to the 50 percent reduction in strategic offensive arms while preserving the 1972 ABM Treaty. Other arms control problems had to be addressed: the elimination of chemical weapons; the reduction of armed forces and conventional armaments in Europe; and the cessation of nuclear testing. In addition, the world was looking to them for "responsible judgments on other complex issues of today"; such as, the settlement of regional conflicts, improving international economic relations, promoting development, overcoming backwardness, poverty, and mass diseases. Almost as an after-thought, he cited "humanitarian problems," the Soviet term for human rights, and bilateral relations.

Previous summits had demonstrated, Gorbachev continued, that "constructive" Soviet-American relations were possible. In his view the INF Treaty was "the most impressive symbol of that." But even more "complex and important tasks lie ahead." Both leaders "still have a lot of work to do" — a human necessity, he philosophized, pledging "to do our utmost" in the negotiations during the coming days in Moscow.

Commenting on the President's past references to the Soviet Union and his interest in Russian proverbs, Gorbachev wanted to add another to his collection: "It is better to see once than to hear a hundred times." The General Secretary assured the President that he could look forward to "hospitality, warmth, and good will." He acknowledged that the Russian people, "full of plans for the future," love their country and take pride in their accomplishments. They resented the obstacles placed in their way and were now "heatedly" discussing how to progress as a nation. As "ardent patriots," they were "open to friendship and cooperation with all nations." He assured the President that they "harbor sincere respect for the American people and want good relations" with their country.

In a peroration, the General Secretary reflected on the setting of the welcoming ceremony within the walls of the ancient Kremlin, "where one feels the touch of history" and where people were moved "to reflect over the diversity and greatness of human civilization." Accordingly, he hoped that this setting would give "greater historical depth" to the talks to be held there "infusing them with a sense of mankind's shared destinies."[66]

c. Reagan's Remarks

In response, the President recalled the previous summit meetings beginning with Geneva in 1985. He acknowledged that they had "faced great obstacles," but by the time of the Washington Summit, where they had to "grapple with difficult issues," they had achieved "impressive progress in all the areas" of their common agenda. He cited in his order of preference, human rights, regional issues, arms reduction and bilateral relations. Specifically, the President mentioned the historic INF Treaty, progress in reducing strategic offensive weapons by 50 percent, and other arms control achievements. "We held full and frank discussions," the President said, "that planted the seeds for future progress."

Summer was approaching and some of those seeds, the President continued, "are beginning to bear fruit, thanks to the hard work" both had done since the Washington Summit, including monthly meetings by the Foreign Ministers and the first meeting of Defense Ministers. He enumerated their success in signing the Geneva accords, providing for withdrawal of Soviet troops from Afghanistan; the conclusion of technical arrangements for implementing the INF Treaty; progress by the negotiators in Geneva on reducing strategic offensive arsenals as recorded in hundreds of pages of joint draft treaty text that designated areas of agreement and disagreement; establishment of the Nuclear Risk Reduction Center; the installation of equipment to verify jointly the limits on nuclear testing; "broad-ranging" discussions on human rights with "important steps" being taken in that area;

and the expansion of bilateral exchanges ("greatly," he said). The President said he could go on — "the list of accomplishments goes far beyond that many anticipated."

The "message is clear," according to Reagan: "despite clear and fundamental differences, and despite the inevitable frustrations that we have encountered, our work has begun to produce results." As if to underscore the deliberate pace of progress, the President cited another Russian proverb: "It was born, it wasn't rushed."

"We did not rush," the President affirmed in conclusion. "We have taken our work step by step," and his presence in Moscow was evidence of his intention of continuing that work. Recalling his departure remarks, he acknowledged the difficulty of the tasks facing them: "It will not be easy." "Tremendous hurdles" have "yet to be overcome." But both leaders had confidence that the task could be accomplished because they shared a "common goal": "Strengthening the framework we have already begun to build for a relationship that we can sustain over the long term — a relationship that will bring genuine benefits to our own peoples and to the world."[67]

3. Opening Discussions in St. Catherine's Hall: "Barbed" Exchange on Human Rights

Differences between Gorbachev and Reagan were submerged in the ceremonial rhetoric of the occasion. But these differences could not long remain hidden beneath the niceties of an official reception as the two leaders went into St. Catherine's Hall in the Kremlin for their first private meeting. Lasting 70 minutes, this meeting became the forum for the first major collision between the General Secretary and the President. The issue was human rights.[68]

On Sunday, the President had presented the General Secretary with a list of 14 cases involving Soviet political prisoners and refuseniks, that is, emigres prevented from leaving Russia. Prior to the first meeting the President was asked by a journalist, presumably a Soviet, if he were posing as a teacher on human rights. He responded, "I have no intention trying to be a teacher."[69]

But that was precisely how the Soviets viewed this matter. For what was described as a "barbed exchange" took place between the two leaders as they defended their respective positions in this first meeting. Gorbachev later made a caustic reference to Reagan's "sermonizing." According to Fitzwater, the President felt that human rights had "pride of place" on the summit agenda because of the high value Americans place on the issue and the concerns of many Americans who trace their roots to Eastern Europe and have been pressuring the Administration to raise the issue at the summit. To Gorbachev this argument, as Howard Baker noted, "strikes sparks."

In an effort to deflect the President's criticism, Gorbachev pointed out that human rights was a "two-way street," according to the Soviet Foreign Ministry spokesman Gennadi I. Gerasimov. The issue was not served well, he said, by a "sensational element and propaganda spirit." He charged that Reagan "does not have a concrete idea, an understanding of where the human rights issue stands with the Soviet Union." Accordingly, Gorbachev proposed establishing a "regular seminar" on human rights between both countries, perhaps at the parliamentary level. According to Fitzwater, the President "responded that he would consider it."[70]

Other general issues were discussed at this first meeting. As Chief of Staff Baker reported over an NBC interview following the first one-on-one meeting, both leaders covered "a wide range of things" from joint space ventures to aspects of regional conflicts. Baker, as others, placed a positive construction on the meeting. There were no surprises, he said, "But the real importance was that these men have developed the ability to communicate and to communicate extensively and, I think, freely between each other....They understand each other remarkably well." Baker felt that the President was "pleased" with the meeting, but he added, "There is a lot of hard work ahead," though he was confident that "it's going to be a good summit."[71]

4.   Walkabout in Arbat Mall

Following the initial meeting with Gorbachev in St. Catherine's Hall, the President went to Spaso House, residence of U.S. Ambassador Jack Matlock, where he stayed during the summit.[72]

A short while later, the Reagans left Spaso House and took an unannounced 10-minute walk through the nearby renovated Arbat pedestrian mall. This was one of the highly visible events that the President's advisers had planned—the White House answer, so to speak, to Gorbachev's seemingly impromptu curbside foray among American onlookers during the Washington Summit.

The Arbat, a sort of Georgetown in Moscow, is a popular meeting and shopping place, crowded with new cafes and boutiques, quick-sketch artists and kitch dealers. Impromptu guitar serenades and occasional displays of "break dancing" provide local color and give an up-beat, easy-going flavor to the place. In brief, Arbat was the ideal colorful setting with Soviets citizens that the President's advisers sought to project around the world, a television image of him talking to and mingling among ordinary Soviet folk.[73]

But the otherwise joyful occasion was marred by the heavy handed Soviet security officials who, apparently fearing for the President's safety, intervened. As the President plunged into the crowded mall, he was immediately surrounded by enthusiastic Moscovites. A pushing match developed between the security officials, reporters and photographers, trying to capture the event for print and film. When the Reagans climbed aboard a painted carriage for photographs and waved to the enthusiastic Soviet crowd, savoring their first close encounter with the Soviet people, the encounter turned ugly. One eyewitness reporter gave this description:

> But the Reagans's delighted smiles gave way to looks of apprehension as Soviet security agents, evidently panicked by the disorder, plunged into the crowd, elbowing and punching, to clear a path to the official limousine that had brought the Reagans from the United States Ambassador's residence a block away. Several reporters trying to follow the Reagans through the crowd said they were hit or kicked, and White House aides exchanged shoves with arm-locked security agents before the Reagans made their exit. Afterward, evidently dazed by the shoving match, the President mustered a chuckle and said, "Someone must have spread the word in advance."[74]

5. Meeting of Working Groups and Foreign Ministers

Less unnerving were the first meetings that evening between U.S. and Soviet working groups. Paul H. Nitze, leading State Department arms negotiator, and Marshal Sergei F. Akromeyev, the Soviet chief of Staff, headed working groups on arms control. Other working groups also met. Rozanne Ridgway and Aleksandr A. Bessmertynk, a Soviet Deputy Foreign Minister, headed working groups that discussed human rights and bilateral issues. Regional conflicts were studied by a group chaired by Assistant Secretary of State Chester A. Crocker and Deputy Foreign Minister Anatoly L. Adamishin.[75]

The working group on arms control, meeting during the evening of the first day, was instructed to report back to their superiors by Tuesday afternoon. American officials considered the naming of Akhromeyev to head the Soviet team as a matter of potentially great significance. For many months they believed that practical compromises were most likely to be forged when the Soviet team was headed by Akromeyev, described as having "unparalleled prestige and authority within his country's military establishment." The Marshal had headed the Soviet arms control working group at Reykjavik where extensive progress was made on detailed issues. Since then, he appeared at several meetings between Gorbachev and Shultz and at the Washington Summit, though he did not play the same direct leadership role among arms specialists as he had at Reykjavik.[76]

During the initial meetings that evening, Soviet officials hinted that they were likely to remove their last-minute roadblocks to completion of a missile-testing notification agreement and annexes to a joint experiment to monitor underground nuclear tests. After hearing their discussion, a U.S. official expressed confidence that those accords would be signed as originally planned later in the week.[77]

In a meeting with Secretary Shultz and other officials, Shevardnadze repeated that the Soviet leadership felt it would be good to conclude a strategic arms treaty with the Reagan Administration if at all possible and was prepared to work hard to accomplish this end.[78]

At such summit meetings Soviet and American officials with common interests often meet outside the framework of the formal conferences. On this first day Secretary of Defense Carlucci and General Dmitri T. Yazov, his Soviet counterpart, conferred informally. Later in a Cable News Network interview, Carlucci acknowledged that while "clearly there's a debate going on" in the Soviet Union about reducing its commitment to an offensive military force, the United States had yet to see any practical effects of that changing doctrine. This new doctrine under debate has been termed "reasonable sufficiency."[79]

6.   An Appraisal of the First Day

The Moscow Summit appeared to get off to a good start. Secretary Shultz remarked that it was "on the whole a good beginning"[80]; the Soviets reaffirmed the judgment of the joint press briefing that it was held "in a serious and businesslike atmosphere and a spirit of goodwill."[81]

The rituals of the formal reception at the airport and the welcoming ceremony in St. George's Hall set the proper tone of mutual respect on both sides and revealed an underlying determination by the President and General Secretary to make the meeting a reasonable success. Collision of views on human rights during the first meeting in St. Catherine's Hall could not be avoided, perhaps only assuaged. The walkabout through Arbat mall provided a portrait for the world of a good-natured, smiling American President engaging in a close encounter with an enthusiastic and friendly Soviet citizenry, marred only by the heavy handed over-reaction of the Soviet security authorities to maintain order. The systemic and philosophical differences between the American democratic style and Soviet authoritarianism were placed in juxtaposition on full display for the world to see. Finally, the structure of the summit was firmly set into place with working groups on both sides meeting to lay out the details of their respective agendas and chart their respective courses of discussion.

B.   SECOND DAY, MONDAY, MAY 30

1.   Gorbachev and Reagan Confer at St. Catherine's Hall

On the second day, the General Secretary and the President conferred for an hour and 45 minutes in St. Catherine's Hall. Meeting in Gorbachev's office at 10:00 a.m., the two leaders proceeded to the Hall for the beginning of talks at 10:15. Despite previous "barbed exchanges" on human rights, both leaders appeared "amiable and relaxed" together during the pre-conference photo opportunity session.[82]

Sources reveal few details of what went on inside the Hall during the discussions at this second meeting. Both leaders were joined by their senior national security advisers including Shultz, Shevardnadze, Carlucci, Soviet Defense Minister Dmitri T. Yazov, Aleksandr N. Yakovlev, one of Gorbachev's closest advisers in the Politburo, and Howard Baker. Presumably, they reviewed in a general way familiar items on the formal agenda, leaving to the working groups the details of the specific negotiations.

2.   Reagan Visits Danilov Monastery

A high point of the second day was the President's visit to the Danilov Monastery located in the southern part of Moscow. The visit coincided with the celebration of the millennium of Russia's conversion to Christianity. A 13th Century Russian Orthodox spiritual and administrative center, the Monastery had been converted to a factory after the Bolshevik Revolution, but in 1983 it was returned to the Church authorities who have undertaken its restoration. During the tour the President was guided by two church leaders, Metropolitan Filaret of Minsk and Archimandrite Tikhon, the dean of the Monastery.[83]

In an address at the Monastery the President placed heavy emphasis on his commitment to religious freedom. He likened the creation and re-creation of the "magnificent icons" he was viewing to the "deep faith that lives in the hearts of the people of this land," a faith that has been "tested and tempered in the crucible of hardship," but in that suffering "has grown strong, ready now to embrace with new hope the beginnings for a second Christian millennium." The President expressed America's hope "for a new age of religious freedom in the Soviet Union." Americans, he said, felt "keenly when religious freedom is denied to anyone anywhere" and hoped that the many Soviet religious communities denied registration or banned altogether would "soon be able to practice their religion freely and openly and instruct their children in and outside the home in the fundamentals of their faith."

The President hoped that perestroika would be accompanied "by a deeper restructuring, a deeper conversion" and "a change in heart" and that glasnost "will also let loose a new chorus of belief, singing praise to the God that gave us life." The President then quoted a passage from Aleksandr Solzhenitsyn, one of Russia's leading writers now living in the United States, to emphasize his point that religious faith was "as elemental to this land as the dark and fertile soil":

When you travel the by-roads of Central Russia, you begin to understand the secret of the pacifying Russian countryside. It is in the churches. They lift their belltowers—graceful, shapely, all different—high over mundane timber and thatch. From villages that are cut off and invisible to each other, they soar to the same heaven. People who are always selfish and often unkind—but the evening chimes used to ring out, floating over the villages, fields and woods, reminding men that they must abandon trivial concerns of this world and give time and thought to eternity.

In a prayerful plea for religious freedom in Russia, the President concluded with the thought that this image be kept in mind: "the thought that the bells may ring again, sounding throughout Moscow and across the countryside, clamoring for joy in their new-found freedom."[84]

3.   Reagan Meets with Dissidents

In further pursuit of his personal agenda, the President met with 98 Soviet dissidents and refuseniks at Spaso House. Prominent among the dissidents and refuseniks were: independent journalists Lev M. Timofeyev and Sergei I. Grigoryants; refuseniks David Schwartzmann and Tanya Zinman; religious activists Father Gleb Yakunin, a Russian Orthodox priest, and Rev. Modris Plate, a Latvian Lutheran minister; and Vyacheslav Chornovil, a Ukrainian human-rights campaigner.[85]

In an address to what was officially termed "selected Soviet citizens," the President conveyed "the prayers and support" of the American people and those throughout the world in hopes that all working for human rights in the Soviet Union "might be encouraged and take heart."

The President called attention to the fact that Americans viewed human rights as "fundamental" to their relationship with the Soviet Union and all nations. From the beginning of his Administration, he said, "we've stressed that an essential element" in improving Soviet-American relations "is human

rights and Soviet compliance with international covenants on human rights."
He acknowledged that there were "hopeful signs," producing, "a hopeful
time for your nation." Americans applauded steps taken so far by the Soviet
leadership, but he stressed that "basic standards" set by the Helsinki Accords and the Universal Declaration of Human Rights "still need to be met."
The President proceeded to lay out the "main aims" of the U.S. human rights
agenda during the Moscow Summit.

The President then made this frank and eloquent explanation of his own
expectations for human rights in the Soviet Union, an explanation, however
appealing to Americans, Gorbachev and his associates no doubt found as
sermonizing and patronizing:

> I've come to Moscow with this human rights agenda because, as I sug-
> gested, it is our belief that this is a moment of hope. The new Soviet
> leaders appear to grasp the connection between certain freedoms and
> economic growth. The freedom to keep the fruits of one's own labor,
> for example, is a freedom that the present reforms seem to be enlarg-
> ing. We hope that one freedom will lead to another and another, that
> the Soviet Government will understand that it is the individual who is
> always the source of economic creativity, the inquiring mind that
> produces a technical breakthrough, the imagination that conceives of
> new products and markets; and that in order for the individual to
> create, we must have a sense of just that — his own individuality, his own
> self-worth. He must sense that others respect him, and, yes, that his
> nation respects him — respects him enough to grant him all his human
> rights. This, as I said, is our hope, yet whatever the future may bring,
> the commitment of the United States will nevertheless remain unshak-
> able on human rights. On the fundamental dignity of the human per-
> son, there can be no relenting, for now we must work for more, always
> more.

Turning to the "personal level," the level of "a fellow human being" from
that of a head of government, and reaching deep into the reservoir of his own
beliefs, the President said he wanted to leave "one thought from my heart,"
and it was his belief that the "history of this troubled century will indeed be
redeemed in the eyes of God and man, and that freedom will truly come to
all." Concluding, he turned to a quote from the 19th Century Russian poet
Pushkin: "It's time, my friend, it's time. The heart begs for peace, "the days
fly past, it's time, my friend, it's time."[86]
In an attempt to counter and possibly embarrass the President, the Soviet-
sponsored Soviet Peace Committee welcomed as visiting "heroes" a group
of American political and social activists. Scarcely known in the United
States these activists and their organizations had been frequently cited in the

Soviet media as representatives of "progressive social forces" in the "land of imperialism." Represented were such groups as the Indian Free Leonard Peltier Committee, the Nuclear Freeze Now Movement, and Children as Peacemakers.

The protesting Americans were given exposure through news conferences and roundtable discussions organized by the Soviet Peace Committee. In the evening the main Soviet television news program, Vremya, screened an interview with the Indians as part of a commentary criticizing Reagan for meeting with the dissidents and refuseniks. Commentator Henryk Borovik said the President could spend his time more profitably by addressing America's own problems rather than lecturing the Soviet Union.[87]

4.   Negotiations on Arms Control

Though irritated by the President's stress on human rights, Gorbachev was no doubt satisfied with discussions on and progress made in arms control. Long discussions on this issue by the two leaders in the morning plus later intensive negotiations by the arms control "working group" led by key defense officials Soviet Marshal Sergei Akhromeyev, Soviet Chief of Staff, and Carlucci in addition to Paul H. Nitze, head of the U.S. negotiating team, resulted in what was described by U.S. and Soviet officials as "unexpected progress on the knotty issue of mobile, land-based strategic nuclear missiles and lesser progress on some other arms issues."[88]

On the basis of a last minute U.S. decision, American negotiators presented a detailed plan to Akhromeyev for limiting and verifying land-based mobile missiles, one of the most vexing arms control issues. After study, the Soviet team responded with their own plan that accepted many of the U.S. points. About 90 percent of the specific issues to be decided on mobile missiles were resolved, according to one official, in the exchange, though, according to other officials, some very important differences on monitoring the perimeter of mobile missile production facilities remained.[89]

Other developments in arms control included: modest progress on air-launched cruise missiles (ALCMs); discussion of the Gorbachev proposal given to Reagan in the morning (unacceptable to the U.S. side in its current form) on reducing conventional arms in Europe, calling for on-site inspection of Warsaw Pact and NATO forces to determine their size and composition and subsequent cuts of 500,000 troops on each side; 11th-hour withdrawal of Soviet demands that threatened to bloc the signing of a U.S.-Soviet agreement that provided for advanced notification of test firings of land-based and submarine-based ICBMs; and Soviet withdrawal of last-minute roadblocks to an accord on a joint experiment to monitor underground nuclear tests.[90]

5. Gorbachev Hosts State Dinner for Reagans

a. Gorbachev's Toast: Realism, Dialogue, Accommodation

The ceremonial highlight of the second day was the state dinner hosted by the Gorbachevs honoring the Reagans in the Kremlin's Faceted Chamber. In a toast, the General Secretary emphasized the importance of the "newly discovered truth that it is no longer possible to settle international dispute by force of arms." Both the Soviets and the Americans, he said, shared this "notion of realism." "Normal, and, indeed, durable Soviet-American relations," he continued, were "only conceivable within the framework of realism." Such a commonly shared belief in realism, he affirmed, had led both countries to the joint conclusion of "historical importance"; namely, "a nuclear war cannot be won and must never be fought."

Talks with Warsaw Pact allies have also shown "a common desire to overcome military confrontation and to end the race in both nuclear and conventional arms." This belief in resolving today's problems solely "by political means is gaining increasing authority" in the world, he said. The trend was towards dialogue, exchanges, for better knowledge and understanding of one another. Making an effort to understand differences did not mean an end to diversity. "The diversity of the world," he declared, "is a powerful wellspring of mutual enrichment, both spiritual and material."

In defense of Soviet policies, the General Secretary explained the importance of perestroika for the "renewal of society," the "humanization of life," and the elevation of ideals. He pledged anew his faith in Socialism. Soviet reforms, he emphasized, called for "more democracy," "more social justice with full prosperity and high moral standards." "Our goal," he asserted in an attempt to counter the President's criticism of Soviet compliance in human rights, "is maximum freedom for man, for the individual, and for society." Gorbachev linked his perception of human rights to "the establishment of a comprehensive system of international security as a condition for the survival of mankind." On issues of peace and progress he asserted his belief in "the primacy of universal human values" and regarded "the preservation of peace as the top priority." In a pledge to the principles of the United Nations, the General Secretary explained:

> We want to build contacts among people in all forums, to expand and improve the quality of information, and to develop ties in the spheres of science, culture, education, sports, and any other human endeavor. But this should be done without interfering in domestic affairs, without sermonizing or imposing one's views and ways, without turning family

or personal problems into a pretext for confrontation between states. In short, our time offers great scope for action in the humanitarian field. Nations should understand each other better, know the truth about each other, and free themselves from bias and prejudice.

Gorbachev enumerated the broad "spectrum of issues," political and economic, that faced the nations of the world. He viewed his policy of "new thinking" as intended to contribute to the solution of these problems and thus far has made possible "a conceptual and practical breakthrough" in Soviet-American relations.

In concluding Gorbachev pointed out that this summit was intended to take stock of the Soviet-American relationship and consolidate "our achievements and give new impetus for the future." He cited progress in arms control and regional issues. But he stressed, as "our main task," the issue of greatest importance to him, the 50 percent reduction in strategic offensive arms, while observing the ABM Treaty. He expressed confidence that the Moscow Summit would "open up new horizons in the Soviet-American dialogue," and this was "worth any effort and any amount of good will."[91]

b.   Reagan's Toast: Friendly Persuasion

The President responded in a toast recalling his meetings with various Soviet people that day and expressing gratitude for the opportunity of meeting "so many divergent members of Soviet society." Such meetings only "confirmed the feelings of admiration and warmth that Americans harbor toward the people of the Soviet Union."

The President recalled the common effort in World War II as wartime allies, and the opportunity this experience gave Americans to "admire the saga of the peoples of the Soviet Union" in building their modern state, in opposing Hitler's armies, and in building a society great in music, architecture, art and literature. Accordingly, the President believed that there existed "common ground between our two peoples," and that it was the duty of both governments "to find common ground as well."

The President observed that he and the General Secretary had much to discuss in the days ahead and that, "What we have achieved is a good beginning." He recounted progress in arms control, in human rights and in building that "network of personal relationships and understanding" between societies and people that "are crucial to dispelling dangerous misconceptions and stereotypes." Both can "take pride" in these "good first steps," he said. But he reiterated that there were areas where more progress should be achieved: in arms control and in fulfilling the goals of the Helsinki Final Act.

On the bilateral level, the President continued, both countries have established the "kind of relationship I think we both had in mind when we first met in Geneva." Both sides have been "candid" about their differences, "sincere" in sharing a common objective, and "working hard together to draw closer to it." Both sides have "gotten into the habit of looking" for those areas of agreement and have "found more than we expected." The President pledged to "pursue the search for common ground" during the remainder of his presidency; he pledged also to tell his successor that "it is a search that must be continued," and based on the achievements of the past three years, he would say that "it is a search that can succeed."

In a long digression in which he alluded to the 1956 Civil War film, "Friendly Persuasion," — a copy of which he gave to an apparently puzzled General Secretary as a gift — to illustrate the problems associated with "the tragedy of war," the "problems of pacifism," "the nobility of patriotism" and the "love of peace," the President drew a parallel between the efforts towards a peaceful settlement in one scene in the film to their pursuit of peace at the summit. On that note of promise and expectations, the President raised his glass and asked that they all "toast the art of friendly persuasion, the hope of peace with freedom, the hope of holding out for a better way of settling things."[92]

6. Reflections on the Second Day

Progress in arms control was apparent during the second day. The arms control working group, supported by the moderately successful negotiations of the principal Soviet and American defense officials, narrowed somewhat the gap of differences. There was some reason for optimism, therefore — but only on the periphery of the arms control talks. Disagreement remained and positions unmovable on the central issue of reducing strategic offensive weapons by 50 percent and finding a mutually acceptable interpretation of the ABM Treaty. Discussions went forward on human rights, bilateral relations and regional issues.

The ceremonial side seemed to serve well the purposes of both the General Secretary and the President. The state dinner in the Kremlin, covered by Soviet television, gave both the opportunity to lay out their conflicting positions on the knotty human rights issue. At the same time each could accent the positive in other aspects of the relationship before a world audience.

Gorbachev proved to be a tough negotiator, formally and in the public forum, particularly on arms control, as he took occasions of high visibility, as at the state dinner, to plead his case openly and forcefully. He was equally unrelenting on human rights as he attempted to give a benign, rational explanation of Soviet policy. On the other hand, he tended to give a positive gloss to Soviet "new thinking" in foreign policy as he linked internal progress in perestroika, glasnost and democratization to peace, world security and the breakthrough in Soviet-American relations. Except for the "sparks" that were generated at the initial meeting with the President and the visible irritation in response to reporter's prodding on human rights, Gorbachev appeared to make his case forcefully and firmly but never with provocation and hostility.

No doubt President Reagan and his advisers found great satisfaction in his performance on the second day. The visit to the Danilov Monastery and the meeting with prominent dissidents at Spaso House, something of a bold master stroke, gave high visibility to his commitment to human rights, and, in general, permitted him to advance his personal agenda on that issue in the best way possible, through words and actions. Both occasions, along with his discreet comments at the state dinner, gave the President a publicly appealing stage—one account referred to the "bully pulpit"—for capturing worldwide attention. While acknowledging the sincerity and eloquence of the President's toast, it was, in addition, a public relations performance of the first magnitude. Yet, he remained firm in his positions, especially on arms control, as he pursued the U.S. agenda.

C.   THIRD DAY, TUESDAY, MAY 31

1.   Gorbachev-Reagan Private Meeting and Stroll Through Red Square

a.   Positive Views on Perestroika and Trade

On Tuesday, May 31, Gorbachev and Reagan began their day with a 10:00 a.m. meeting at the General Secretary's private office in the Kremlin. At this third meeting the President, avoiding the human rights issue that stirred deep negative reactions within his interlocutor, placed special emphasis in their talks on encouraging positive change in the Soviet Union through perestroika. The meeting was scheduled to last 15 minutes but was expanded with only interpreters and notetakers present to more than an hour. The discussion focused principally on perestroika and Gorbachev's domestic programs. "It was all domestic, philosophical, political," said Fitzwater later. "The President wanted to give Gorbachev a chance to talk about perestroika."[93]

Prospects for major increases in Soviet-American economic ties were also examined by the two leaders. As the President later told students at Moscow State University,

Nothing would please my heart more than in my lifetime to see American and Soviet diplomats grappling with the problem of trade disputes [rather than military disputes] between America and a growing, exuberant, exporting Soviet Union that opened up to economic freedom and growth.[94]

The President's expressed pleasure at trade expansion seemed to mark a 180 degree reversal from his position six years ago when he angered U.S. Allies by pressuring them not to participate in building a Soviet natural gas pipeline to Western Europe.

On his part, Gorbachev urged expanded trade which he linked to his belief in global interdependence and improving prospects for better political relations. As he later told reporters: "If there are good economic and trade relations, we become more and more dependent on each other. And this in turn makes us more predictable."[95]

b.   Irritation and Discord on Arms Control

Yet all was not tranquil at this morning meeting. Gorbachev, pushing his arms control agenda, voiced his displeasure at the slow pace of progress in arms negotiations in a meeting with reporters prior to their one-on-one session in the General Secretary's office. Referring to their talks the previous day on a wide range of arms control issues and expressing confidence in the progress previously made by their negotiators, the General Secretary believed that there "will be more progress after that conversation." Prodding Reagan a bit, he went on to say that if the President "makes effective use of the remaining time, we will still be able to prepare that treaty" – the treaty on reducing strategic offensive weapons. The President agreed. When asked if he thought the treaty were possible, Gorbachev replied, "If you ask me, I think it is possible" – again an affirmative response from the President. Venting his clear displeasure at the slow pace of the negotiations, the General Secretary complained:

You know, the President and I have had situations where we were in a kind of impasse. And I remember a time in Geneva [during their first summit meeting in 1985] when the President said: "In the end, let's bang our fists on the table." I said: "Yes, let's." By morning we had agreed [to] everything, and successfully completed Geneva. Perhaps the time is now approaching when we should bang our fists on the table again?

Did the President agree with this remark? "Yes," he said, "if it helps."[96]

c.   Strolling Through Red Square

A highlight of the morning schedule was a stroll through Red Square. Secretary Shultz had told Reagan about Red Square, and the President wanted to see it and so asked the General Secretary if "he could take me by for a look."[97] In what was described as "shirtsleeve weather" (close to 80 degrees), the President and the General Secretary emerged from their third private meeting through an ancient gate of the Kremlin to begin a 20-minute stroll together through Red Square. The broad cobblestone square where military reviews and celebrations take place on state occasions was cleared of all but a few knots of people.[98]

Both leaders took full advantage of this remarkable setting to put the finest gloss on this summit and their respective purposes. "We want our children to live in peace," said a woman holding a small child. Gorbachev took the child into his arms and said, "shake hands with Grandfather Reagan." The picture of this incident conveyed to the world what both leaders had sought, a sense of humanity cherished by both peoples and the expressed desire, reflected in this portrait, to search for peace through dialogue. Fitzwater may have best summed up this event when he later responded to a query as to what was most significant for the President at the summit:

> Well, the president commented at some point in the course of the tour of Red Square that we're talking to each other and not about each other.... Probably the most dramatic impact that has occurred here has been the interaction with the people and the feeling that has developed between the delegations that we can do business.[99]

The stroll provided the President another chance to comment favorably on the Soviet women. "I have great admiration for the women of Russia," he said to a mostly female group, echoing a point he made a week ago in an interview over Soviet television. "You are so courageous and contribute so much to the whole society."[100]

Someone in a group of Soviets at one side of this vast square raised the question of space cooperation. Fulfilling an earlier promise to bring up this matter, Gorbachev proposed to Reagan that both nations "launch a mission to Mars together." "Our space people are looking into this subject," the President replied, noting that the 1986 Challenger disaster had set back the American space program. "But this will be in several phases," Gorbachev persisted, citing as evidence the plan for unmanned missions to Mars and later manned missions. Apparently not receiving a further explanation, the General Secretary commented that Reagan "is being a little cautious."[101]

In one instance Gorbachev turned to a small boy in the crowd and asked, "What do you thing about the President's visit to us? What do you think of it? Is it a good thing?" Ruffling the boy's hair as he received a reply, the General Secretary put it in his own words: ". . .it was a very good thing, as it was for the sake of peace, at any rate, to get a higher level of mutual understanding between our two countries." The President injected his own observations on the visit, voicing a key principle of his policy: "What we decided to do is to talk to each other instead of about each other." Gorbachev responded, "Yes," and the President countered, "That is working just fine."[102]

When asked later on if he still thought the Soviet Union is "the Evil Empire," the President responded categorically, "No."[103] "I was talking about another time, another era," he added.[104]

2. Reagan's Luncheon with Soviet Intellectuals

a. The Setting

The next stop on Reagan's busy schedule was a luncheon in his honor with 38 Soviet intellectuals at the Central House of Writers. Recall that Gorbachev had a similar meeting with American intellectuals during the Washington Summit. Unlike the splendid, sweeping panorama of a near empty Red Square, the Writer's House provided a more constricted, confining setting, one having the intimacy and camaraderie of a prestigious men's club, ideal for group interaction and for influencing a powerful Soviet elite as this group of intellectuals represented. For in the communist world, writers are not just literary entertainers but are rather another "estate" of power for shaping their nation's destiny. Reagan's planners clearly had this in mind when they scheduled the luncheon.

b. Welcoming by Soviet Cultural Leaders

The President met with some of the Soviet Union's leading cultural figures — writers, artists, filmmakers and intellectuals — and lunched in the paneled dining room of the Writer's House. Speaking for the Soviet "creative intelligentsia," writer Sergy Zalygin, filmmaker Elem Klimov, and the painter Andrei Vasnetsov addressed the President. All spoke of the community of all people that is inherent in the arts and called attention to its "enormous moral potential" for encouraging peace and progress.

Recalling the inter-relationship between writers, political power and exercising political influence in society, Vladimir Karpov, head of the official writer's union, emphasized that throughout mankind's history writers have played a role in determining the fate of states and individual people. He underscored the dangers besetting mankind in the Nuclear Age, praised the Soviet policy of "new thinking" for its positive impact on insuring world peace, and acknowledged that the President's pronouncements "inspire hope that reason will triumph and accord be reached." Knowing the President's attachment to Russian proverbs, Karpov recited one "as a memento," he said, of the meeting and of the work being done at this summit, "Start well and you are half way there."[105]

c.   Reagan Addresses Intellectuals

In his brief remarks, President Reagan acknowledged Russia's historic contribution to the arts, greeting the Soviet intellectuals as "heirs to the seminal figures in many of the arts as they have developed in 20th Century Europe and America," figures like Stravinsky, Stanislavsky and Dostoyevsky, "to name a few men whose vision transformed all of ours." Alluding to the "indispensable" lessons gained in acting that prepared him for the Presidency, the President recalled the words of Eisenstein, the noted Soviet film director, who said during the production of his classic, "Ivan the Terrible,"

The most important thing is to have the vision. The next is to grasp and hold it. You must see and feel what you are thinking. You must see and grasp it. You must hold and fix it in your memory and senses. And you must do it at once.

The "very essence" of "successful leadership," the President explained, expanding on a metaphorical theme linking art and politics, is "to grasp and hold a vision, to fix it in your senses." Not only did he learn this lesson "on the movie set" but "everywhere." Alluding to his "many dealings" with Gorbachev, Reagan declared that the General Secretary "has the ability to grasp and hold a vision, and I respect him for that."

Having established the point that success in political leadership requires, as in acting, the ability "to grasp and hold a vision," the President explained the "second lesson" that he carried with him in the transition from acting to public life. He referred to the Soviet poet Anna Akhmatova—"one of the world's greatest," he said—who at the beginning of "Requiem" writes of standing in a line outside a prison and being asked by an inmate, "Can you describe this?"—and she answered, "I can."

That exchange, the President said, revealed "the heart of acting, as it is of poetry and of so many of the arts," because they require getting "inside a character, a place and a moment." In acting, he continued, one becomes "more attentive to the core of the soul—that part of each of us that God holds in the hollow of his hand, and into which he breathes the breath of life." The President believed that political leadership in a democracy requires,

> seeing past the abstractions and embracing the vast diversity of humanity, and doing it with humility; listening as best you can, not just to those with high positions, but to the cacophonous voices of ordinary people, and trusting those millions of people, keeping out of their way; not trying to act the all-wise and all-powerful; not letting government act that way. And the word we have for this is freedom.

The President acknowledged approvingly the expansion of freedom in the arts in the Soviet Union during the last few years, a point well received by the audience. "We in the United States applaud the new thaw in the arts," he said. "We hope to see it go further," and he continued, suggesting the connection between freedom, peace and progress:

> We want this not just for your sake, but for our own. We believe that the greater the freedoms in our countries, the more secure both our own freedoms and peace. And we believe that when the arts in any country are free to blossom, the lives of all people are richer.

d. Favorable Reaction from Soviet Audience

After the President's luncheon meeting ended, Roy A. Medvedev, an historian with a dramatist's eye, noticed an essential paradox. "All of our artists spoke like politicians," he said, "and the politician, Mr. Reagan, spoke like an actor." In a society where performance in the theater, poetry and cinema is often considered a more genuine form of political expression than politics itself and coming from an intellectual whose words have been banned by the politicians, "this is no belittling remark," wrote Bill Keller, Moscow correspondent for The New York Times. According to Keller, the President had "connected" with his audience in what was described as a "bravura" performance.[106]

Though visibly tired and sometimes dozing as some Soviet speakers droned on, the President reportedly impressed his audience very favorably by his sincerity and personal warmth, his compassion for artistic freedom and profound insight into the relationship between the arts, the freedom of the artist and progress of civilization. Playing what was described as "his accustomed role of the modest, personable, former actor," Reagan inspired this comment from Fedor Burlatsky, editor of Moscow's Literary Gazette, leading reformer and close adviser of Gorbachev's: "I think the president gave one of the best speeches of his life. He spoke very sincerely, he mentioned all those names that are very dear to the Russian intelligentsia." To Zalygin, it was "a very artistic, delicate speech"[107] – an appraisal shared no doubt by many others within the Soviet cultural elite.

3.   Reagan Addresses Students and Faculty at Moscow State University

a.   The Setting

A high point in the President's third day in Moscow was his address to some 600 students and faculty members at Moscow State University, the alma mater of both Gorbachev and his wife. The marble hall was packed; students, unable to get seats, stacked chairs, tables and desks in the corridors and climbed on top of them, hoping to get a glimpse of the American President. The President had, therefore, a large, prime-quality audience, attentive and interested, inquisitive and acquisitive, one not to be won over, but to be influenced.

Reagan's performance at the Soviet Union's most prestigious university was regarded by his White House planners as the centerpiece of his campaign to reach out to the Soviet people and encourage the forces of change unleashed by Gorbachev. The objective was to appeal to the young and creative minds of Soviet students, the future leaders in Soviet society; to inspire them by a positive appraisal of changes now underway and by portraying a larger and more creative vision of freedom; and to influence them as a hedge against any possible reversal of course in the future. In brief, to help insure that Gorbachev's changes will survive, while attempting to project the best of the American philosophical and institutional reality.

As the President gave his formal address (very long, it might be added) and responded to a mixture of curious and critical questions for about 20 minutes, he stood in front of a vast mosaic filled with surging red flags of revolution; a large white marble bust of Lenin looked sternly down on the proceedings from above his head. The setting and the President's purposes were in marked contrast to his discourse on the "evil empire" before a gathering of American evangelists early in his First Administration.[108]

b.   His Message, "A Lesson in American Civics"

The President's speech was aptly described as "a lesson in American civics"; for that is precisely what it was as he examined not just the "realities of today" but the "possibilities of tomorrow." He elaborated on the "technological or information revolution" now underway globally, symbolized by "the tiny silicon chip," and its impact on the world today. Noting the importance of the spiritual dimension of society, he assured his young listeners that "progress is not foreordained" unless it is driven by the deeper forces of freedom. "The key is freedom," the President affirmed, "freedom of thought, freedom of information, freedom of communication."

The President explained at length the virtues of democracy in the political, economic, cultural and legal spheres, pointing out the value of freedom as a liberating and creative force for mankind. "Freedom is the right to question and change the established way of doing things," he said, by way of example. "It is the continuing revolution of the marketplace," meaning a free and continuous exchange of ideas in the forum of public discourse.

Turning to the positive changes taking place within Soviet society, Reagan cautioned that "reform that is not institutionalized will always be insecure." Hence in talks with the General Secretary he emphasized "how important it is to institutionalize change — to put guarantees on reform."

The President reviewed the progress made thus far in Soviet-American relations, progress, he said, "few would have imagined" just a few years ago. Addressing the deeper ideological conflict, he emphasized that, "Peace between nations must be an enduring goal, not a tactical stage in a continuing conflict," a cardinal principle in Soviet foreign policy during the days before Gorbachev. He looked forward to further improvements in Soviet-American relations in the belief, as he said many times before, that, "People do not make wars, governments do." And he cited such areas for future progress as in trade expansion and an increase in people-to-people exchanges.

Addressing specifically the youth of Russia and the future, the President declared that, "Your generation is living in one of the most exciting, hopeful times in Soviet history." "It is a time," the President explained, "when the first breath of freedom stirs the air and the heart beats to the accelerated rhythm of hope, when the accumulated spiritual energies of a long silence yearn to break free."

The President concluded with this peroration, expressing uncertainty for the future but a promise of hope for the fulfillment of reform:

> We do not know what the conclusion will be of this journey, but we're hopeful that the promise of reform will be fulfilled. In this Moscow spring, this May 1988, we may be allowed that hope — that freedom, like the fresh green sapling planted over Tolstoy's grave — will blossom forth at last in the rich fertile soil of your people and culture. We may be allowed to hope that the marvelous sound of a new openness will keep rising through, ringing through to a new world of reconciliation, friendship, and peace.[109]

c.   Reactions from the Soviet Audience

In his performance at Moscow University, President Reagan played the role of a super-salesman for freedom, preaching in effect that freedom was the driving force carrying modern nations into the Third Wave of world civilization; namely, the Scientific-Technological Age of the 21st Century. His was a plea for the Soviet Union to join the ranks, as Gorbachev was beckoning them, to be a part of this global revolution and to institutionalize what achievements have been made thus far. Sometimes eloquent, sometimes the didactic teacher, but always in the style of the "soft-sell" salesman (there was no overt criticism of the Soviet Union or sharp rhetoric), he made a strong and appealing case before this bright, tough, critical but reflective audience. Accordingly, the President, relying on his gifts as "a great communicator" "pulled out all the stops," so to speak, displaying an appealing charm. As one correspondent reported: "As he has so often on the hustings in his own country, Mr. Reagan charmed the audience, which repeatedly applauded his answers and gave him a standing ovation even if they did not accept all his arguments."[110]

But beneath his charm there was seen an unexpected intelligence and vision of the future. This select Soviet audience was described as attentive and impressed, but no doubt remained wary. They liked the President personally but dissented from many of his ideas. "It was great, for the first time, to see the President," said Pyotr Skorospelov, a student of American history. "His speech was very good." But he disagreed with Reagan's emphasis on human rights, a major theme of his Moscow visit. "It is his right to say such things," Skorospelov said outside the lecture hall. "But it is also our right to go our own way."[111]

One by one as the students emerged from the hall many acknowledged that the speech had altered their stereotype of the President as a strident anti-Communist portrayed in the Soviet media. Anatoly Cherasksky, a 25 year old physics major, expected "the worst" anti-Communist rhetoric, a confused worldview and antagonism toward Russians, "But it wasn't like that at all." He gave this appraisal: "His position was not at all confused. It had a certain logic to it. He seems to have a vision for world peace and he wants young people to help bring it about. It liked it. I like him now, too."

Vladimir Berezdvin, an 18 year old geography major sporting long hair, faded jeans and a T-shirt, offered this assessment: "It's not very often that we have such a major world leader talking in practical terms like that. You could really grasp, really understand what he was talking about. I will never think that Reagan is superficial again."[112]

And Andrei Fronin, a 25 year old political science major, observed that, "It was not the Reagan that we expected. There was nothing old-fashioned or stale about him. He seemed to be so lively, active and thinking. This was a pleasant surprise.[113]"

Thus the President appeared to have made a substantial impact on this young elite audience. As one correspondent observed: "With similarly warm reviews of the speech sweeping across the elite university's sprawling campus, Reagan appeared to make remarkably swift headway in influencing one of the most important groups in the Soviet Union."[114]

The President's advisers in the White House were no doubt pleased by this success, but there could be only little satisfaction in knowing that only "snippets" of the address were broadcast over Soviet television to a wider Soviet audience.

4. Reagans Host State Dinner for Gorbachevs

a. The Setting

The last strictly ceremonial function of the third day was the state dinner at Spaso House, the U.S. Ambassador's residence, hosted by the Reagans honoring the Gorbachevs. During the day Mrs. Reagan had toured Leningrad, returning to Moscow in time for the dinner. About 120 Soviet and American guests attended including, in addition to leading Soviet officials and senior members of the U.S. summit contingent, U.S. Senate leaders Robert C. Byrd (D-W.Va.), Majority Leader, and Robert Dole (R-Kan.), Minority Leader, both of whom arrived in Moscow that day having concluded Senate ratification of the INF treaty; Soviet dissidents Andrei D. Sakharov and his wife Yelena G. Bonner; British composer Andrew Lloyd Webber; and American jazz pianist Dave Brubeck, who entertained at the dinner. Most guests outside the political, military and diplomatic spheres were Soviet intellectuals, artists and athletes.[115]

b. The President's Toast

In his toast the President compared their springtime Moscow Summit with previous ones held in the autumn, the former being "a time of long, light-filled days," the latter, "the weather ever grayer and colder" — a metaphorical allusion, presumably, to the improving political environment. He reviewed the importance of Spaso House in Soviet-American relations, noting particularly the "unnaturally quiet times" when relations were difficult.

Speaking of the state of affairs today, the President acknowledged that on "matters of great importance, we will continue to differ profoundly." Yet, they had met four times, more often than any previous President and General Secretary. Their negotiations were sometimes "pointed or contentious," still, accenting and positive, "we possess an enlarged understanding of each other and each other's country." The President affirmed that on specific matters of policy, "we have made progress—often historic progress," adding: "And perhaps most important, we have committed our nations to continuing to work together, agreeing that silence must never again be permitted to fall between us."

Success in the relationship and the mutual pledge to continuing interchanges, the President declared, were rooted in the belief that "we both hear the same voice, the same overwhelming imperative." Quoting Boris Pasternak's poem, "The Garden of Gethsemane," and alluding to the scene when Peter cut off the ear of an intruding religious adversary, the President quoted Christ's command, "Put your sword in its place, O man." "This is the imperative, the command," he said. "And so," he pledged, "we will work together, that we might forever keep our swords at our sides."[116]

c.   The General Secretary's Toast

In a responding toast, the General Secretary reviewed the course of Soviet-American relations, candidly acknowledging the good times and the bad. The Geneva Summit marked the beginning of an era when both countries sought to "overcome a long drawn out period of confrontation" and reach an "acceptable level from which is now easier to move forward." In their meetings at the summit, including Moscow, Gorbachev stated frankly, "our dialogue has been intense." But he pointed to the "most important result," the signing of the INF Treaty, among others: progress in reducing strategic offensive weapons; the accord on Soviet withdrawal from Afghanistan; and the fact that 47 bilateral agreements on cooperation were in force.

The main tendency in world developments, Gorbachev went on, is the "turning toward a search for political solutions, toward cooperation and peace." Momentous changes have occurred, but "a lot still has to be done to achieve irreversible change." Despite cooperation and growing trust, "prejudices and stereotypes are still with us, as is rivalry, above all in the military sphere." Nonetheless, at this summit, "we can register some headway toward better mutual understanding in this area as well."

The General Secretary then proceeded to share his views with the President on problems in the Third World and to reflect on the state of Soviet-American bilateral relations. Gorbachev called for a solution of Third World problems (which he cited as, "glaring backwardness," hunger, poverty, mass diseases and an "incredibly high debt") by a "radical restructuring of the entire system of world economic relations, without any discrimination for political reasons." Such a course would "promote a political settlement of regional conflicts" that impede progress in the Third World and cause "turmoil in the entire world situation."

Addressing the subject of bilateral relations, Gorbachev recalled how both sides are studying developments and trends in their respective countries. Differences abound in both systems, he readily acknowledged, but such societal differences are not "an obstacle to identifying promising areas for mutually beneficial ties or for cooperation" in the interests of both countries. "We're in favor of composition and comparison," he added.

Gorbachev observed how Soviet and American representatives have been upholding their state interests despite the ups and downs in the dialogue. But these state interests can only be achieved when both sides view the relationship realistically and take into account each other's interests and intentions. Accordingly, he concluded, "We must learn the difficult art of not just existing side by side, but of building bridges of mutually beneficial cooperation."

The General Secretary then gave his vision of the future, a future in which both countries "base their relations on disarmament, a balance of interest, and comprehensive cooperation rather than deterring each other or upgrading their military capabilities." Solutions to real problems in this future will no longer be impeded by problems "historically outdated or artificially kept alive" by the inheritances of the Cold War. Policies of confrontation will "give way to a joint quest based on reason, mutual benefit, and readiness to compromise."

Gorbachev envisioned a future in which both countries, not claiming any special rights in the world, "are always mindful of their special responsibility in a community of equal nations." The world will be safer and more secure, he said, a world within which all peoples can "gain and preserve the basic human rights: the right to life, work, freedom and the pursuit of happiness."

The path towards achieving this vision "can be neither easy nor short," the General Secretary cautioned. But he believed, nonetheless, that both nations "may be standing at the threshold of a uniquely interesting period in the history of our two nations." Gorbachev did not doubt that this meeting in Moscow "confirms that 3 years ago in Geneva, we took the right decision."[117]

d.   Sentimentalism and Realism

At first glance the President's toast seemed to contain two essential ingredients reflecting his approach to the Soviets thus far in the Moscow Summit. As an actor fascinated by a good script and an appealing dramatic setting, Reagan gave a high gloss of sentimentalism to his remarks, particularly in his biblical reference to the futility of attempting to solve world problems by the sword. Yet beneath this gloss lies the idea that despite incidence of "pointed or contentious" dialogue progress has been made in a relationship based on a common commitment to negotiations and diplomacy, based on the hard power realities of international life, that will insure peace between both countries. This suggests a subtle but effective mixture of sentimentalism and realism.

In contrast, Gorbachev's toast seems firmly planted in the hard political realities of the superpower relationship. Absent from his remarks is any literary allusion that suggests sentimentalism, though his vision of the future suggests an element of idealism present in the Soviet reality. Rather, Gorbachev begins from the basic premise in international relations; namely, the necessity of realism and the necessity of taking into account each other's interests and intentions as the baseline (or "the bottom line") of a relationship. From this baseline he moves to the next logical level of "building bridges of mutually beneficial cooperation" as a means for achieving those mutual interests.

Thus, while both leaders approach the relationship from different perspectives, they arrive at a common point through realism, differently projected, but realism nonetheless.

5.   Formal Signing of Agreements

a.   Success on Minor Accords; Deadlock on Strategic Arms Reduction

On the third day Soviet and American negotiators approved nine agreements. The practical diplomatic business of the Moscow Summit was going forward with some success. Two of the nine, pertaining to arms control, were signed by Shevardnadze and Shultz during the morning session with Gorbachev and Reagan witnessing the signings but not taking part in the ceremony because they were considered minor. As Soviet Foreign Ministry spokesman Gerasimov remarked, the agreements "are too small for them." "It's important," he said, "but not that important."[118] One of the arms control agreements required advance notification on launchings of ballistic missiles; the other provided for experiments to improve the means for monitoring limits on nuclear testing. The signing took place in the red sitting room of the Grand Kremlin Palace; the proceedings were carried over Soviet television.[119] Considered a ritual for such summit meetings, the signing ceremony was intended to suggest progress in Soviet-American relations, even though no breakthroughs were reported on a strategic arms treaty.

Because the Gorbachev-Reagan morning meeting had exceeded the allotted time, Shevardnadze and Shultz met with senior aides in order to make a final effort to overcome some of the remaining obstacles to agreement on strategic arms control. "Rumors of progress swirled through the press corps," one journalist reported, "but one American official said there was no basis to them."[120] Soviet Defense Minister Dmitri T. Yazov and U.S. Defense Secretary Carlucci also met again, but without reports of a breakthrough, there was little expectation that a treaty reducing strategic or intercontinental weapons could be completed before Reagan's term expired. Nonetheless, both leaders continued to express hope that they would make progress.[121]

The seven other agreements that were signed by the foreign secretaries covered a wide range of issues. One called for the limited exchange program of Soviet and American students to be expanded from the maximum of 50 to 1,500 students for the next two years. Other agreements expanded Soviet-American cooperation in nuclear-power research and provided for limited cooperation in space exploration. The remaining accords related to maritime search and rescue, fisheries, transportation and radio navigation.[122]

b.   Progress on Angolan Issue

Notable progress was made in negotiations on the Angolan issue. Soviet and American negotiators, Adamishin and Crocker, met as a separate working group in tandem with the main summit proceedings. Agreement was reached in principle that Cuban forces should be withdrawn from Angola over the next 12 months. These talks produced a much faster timetable than the one proposed by the Soviet-supported Government of Angola. Previously they had insisted that only half of the Cuban forces could be withdrawn in two years and that it would require four years for the final departure of the Cuban troops. Gorbachev and Reagan were expected to discuss Southern Africa and other regional conflicts at their final scheduled meeting on Wednesday, June 1.[123]

6.   Reflections on the Third Day

a.   Triumph of Public Diplomacy

The third day of the Moscow Summit proved to be a triumph of public diplomacy for both Gorbachev and Reagan. The stroll through Red Square, the ceremonial toasts and the personal interaction with guests at the Spaso House state dinner, and the informal press conferences – all gave the General Secretary great opportunities for publicly advancing his agenda. For him the third day was a triumph for glasnost, a new openness in dialogue with the Soviet and world public. At times of maximum exposure over television the General Secretary, always affable and charming but still directly and firmly to the point, was also able to reiterate his confidence in diplomatic dialogue and negotiations with the United States and outline important areas of agreement in economic, cultural, scientific and political relations as well as in minor areas of arms control. But at the same time he was able to give his interpretation of disagreements as in the case of strategic arms reductions where Soviet and American differences have thus far proved to be irreconcilable.

The third day was even more so a triumph in public diplomacy for President Reagan. No American President has ever had such a choice opportunity for reaching out to and influencing the Soviet people as had Reagan during his televised walk through Red Square and addresses at the Writer's House and Moscow University. By Soviet acknowledgment the President's addresses touched very positive chords with this Soviet elite. His audience may not have been convinced of his case for democracy American style, but his message about intellectual freedom as a driving force of progress in a technological-scientific civilization cannot have failed to make a deep impression on them. Important also was the President's support for Gorbachev's reform policies, and particularly noteworthy was his emphasis on the need for institutionalizing reform to insure its durability.

For both leaders, therefore, the third day produced many positive and satisfying results. Public diplomacy and summitry were well served.

b.   Failure in Strategic Arms Reduction

The negative side of the third day was failure in arms control. Minor successes were registered by the signing of agreements on such matters as nuclear testing and in the area of cultural affairs and scientific cooperation. Progress on the Angolan issue also proved to be highly important. But solutions to the major issue, reduction of strategic weapons, continued to escape the negotiators.

After three days of negotiations in Moscow there was no sign of a breakthrough on the key issues blocking a strategic arms agreement. The Soviets voiced disappointment that U.S. negotiators did not bring new ideas on the two principal areas of contention: the Strategic Defense Initiative (SDI) and the sea-launched cruise missiles (SLCMs). "We would like the American delegation to originate new, fresh ideas" and "show a readiness for discussion," said Ministry of Foreign Affairs spokesman Gerasimov. "With SLCMs, where the American side does not want to meet our expectations, no doubt we have a certain element of disappointment."[124]

Substantial progress had been made toward a treaty on the reduction of strategic arms. Recall that at Reykjavik in 1986, negotiators on both sides agreed to limit strategic weapons to 6,000, approximately a 50 percent reduction, and strategic missile launchers and bombers to 1,600. Agreement had also been reached on limiting warheads on land- and sea-based ballistic missiles to 4,800. Deadlock continued, nonetheless, notably on the most difficult issue of establishing limits on SLCMs. The United States, ahead in guidance and propulsion systems for such missiles, eventually planned to deploy about 4,000 missiles. The Soviets, concerned by this development, has wanted to establish verifiable limits on SLCMs. One knotty issue was how to distinguish between nuclear-armed and conventionally armed versions of the missiles.[125]

The other issue blocking agreement was how much testing was permissible for SDI under the 1972 ABM treaty. At the Washington Summit in December 1988, both sides adopted what was described as "a vague, highly contorted formula" for resolving the problem which allowed each side to conduct testing it believed necessary under the ABM Treaty. The problem arose from Soviet insistence on a strict interpretation of the treaty, while the United States adopted a "broad" or "loose" interpretation that would permit SDI testing outside the laboratory.[126]

Other issues remained unresolved, and it was on these that the negotiators hoped to make progress in Moscow. One was how to limit air-launched cruise missiles, and how to count them aboard bombers. The Soviets proposed that each bomber be counted as carrying as many ALCMs as its capacity would allow. The United States has sought to limit the count to 10, on grounds that the slow-flying cruise missiles were not as threatening as fast-flying ballistic missiles.[127]

The summit negotiators were also trying to make headway on mobile land-based missiles. The United States had proposed a ban on such missiles but was expected to abandon its position in light of the Department of Defense's interest in deploying rail-based MX missiles. Other issues included sublimits on ICBM warheads and the complex problem of on-site verification of a strategic arms reduction treaty.[128]

"Because of these sticky issues," writes Charlotte Saikowski of The Christian Science Monitor from Moscow, "many American arms experts are dubious that a strategic arms reduction treaty can be completed before the end of the Reagan Administration. But both American and Soviet officials continue to voice hope that an agreement can be reached this year."[129]

c.   Favorable Signs

Diplomatic observers at the Moscow Summit were not at all surprised by the absence of any new U.S. initiative to break the deadlock in arms control. As they approached the Moscow Summit, high American officials had conspicuously indicated their failure to establish a unified Administration position on START. Nonetheless, throughout the third day there were positive signs: Shevardnadze and Shultz held extensive talks in the morning; Carlucci and his Soviet counterpart Yazov met again for two and one-half hours to discuss, among other things, START verification problems; and Gorbachev and Reagan persisted in their intention of keeping the momentum going on the arms control dialogue, even though no immediate breakthrough seemed likely on the horizon. Spokesmen for both sides were, nonetheless, restrained in their predictions. Fitzwater said the United States would like to sign a treaty during this administration and "will be working toward that goal." Gerasimov believed this was possible, given the "political will" and if both sides "roll up their sleeves."[130]

Soviet political commentator, prominent reformer and adviser to the leadership Alexander Bovin struck a more optimistic note. Speaking of the Moscow Summit as a whole, he told the listening Soviet television audience,

> So there are some positive changes. They don't go very deep as yet, but they are happening. It's like the hand of a clock: When you look at it, it appears to be standing still, but just look away for a moment, and it's moved. That's what's happening here too.

And he reminded his Soviet listeners,

> This is a beginning, the beginning of a long road. But it indeed seems that the cold war is, thank God, receding despite everything. It has given in its positions. And this breakthrough has [...produced] a qualitatively new meaning now in world politics as a whole.[131]

D.   FOURTH DAY, WEDNESDAY, JUNE 1

1.   Formal Exchange of INF Instruments of Ratification

a.   The Formal Setting in Vladimir Hall

It was a very tired President Reagan who met with the ebullient and energetic General Secretary at 10:00 a.m. in Vladimir Hall of the Grand Kremlin Palace to exchange the INF instruments of ratification formally putting into force the first treaty to require the destruction of nuclear weapons, in this case intermediate-range and shorter-range missiles. The First Ladies spent their morning touring the Tretyakov Gallery.[132]

What made the signing ceremony distinctive was the fact that the 1979 SALT II Treaty and the 1974 test ban treaties were never ratified by the Senate and thus never formally went into force, though both sides pledged to abide by SALT II. It was fitting, therefore, that standing by observing the final proceedings were Senate Majority Leader Robert C. Byrd (D-W.Va.)

and Minority Leader Robert Dole (R-Kan.) who led the Senate in giving its final approval on the previous Friday.[133]

By tradition, Soviet leaders sign the most important international agreements concluded at the summit level in Vladimir Hall. When Gorbachev and Reagan appeared, Soviet and American officials applauded. At what the Soviets described as "a solemn moment," both leaders took their seats at the table, flanked by two aides, and signed the protocols on the exchange of instruments of ratification. Again the official audience applauded. After the signing, first Gorbachev and then Reagan addressed the audience. The proceedings were recorded over Soviet television.[134]

b. Gorbachev's Remarks: Opening Era of Nuclear Disarmament

In a clearly expansive and optimistic mood, the General Secretary began by affirming that the exchange of these instruments of ratification means that "the era of nuclear disarmament has begun." In assessing the tasks undertaken at this Moscow Summit, Gorbachev expressed his satisfaction, noting particularly that what was happening during these few days was "big politics," meaning, "politics that affect the interests of millions and millions of people." With each summit, Soviet and American negotiators have "dealt a blow at the foundation of the cold war." Each summit had made "huge breaches in the cold war fortress and opened up passages to modern, civilized world politics worthy of the truly new times."

"Big politics," Gorbachev continued, however uplifting and praiseworthy, had its down side. It means "difficult politics in which every step is not easy to take." Achievements are measured, he went on, against the security interests of both nations and the world at large, for that is "the only way to achieve truly substantial results with the necessary margin of viability."

"Big politics" means "big responsibility," and, accordingly, it cannot be carried forth solely on the pursuit of "only one's own interest" which is "always inherently one-sided." "Big politics" also needs "a great idea," and for the Soviet Union it was "the idea of a nuclear-free and nonviolent world." This idea, Gorbachev affirmed, is a mandate for all Soviet negotiators, especially when negotiating with the United States. Accordingly, Gorbachev solemnly pledged to all the world that the Soviet Union has been "working honestly and with perseverance" and shall continue to do so in fulfilling "that historic mandate."

Using the metaphor of a book, the General Secretary declared that in this INF Treaty the first lines have been written into "the book of a world without wars, violence, or nuclear weapons," a cardinal principle of his foreign policy. No one can close that book, he said, and "put it aside." Both he and President Reagan had agreed that the immediate task before them now was to conclude a treaty reducing strategic offensive arms by 50 percent. This goal, he emphasized, "must and can be accomplished." Accenting the positive, Gorbachev acknowledged that in their negotiations both leaders "have learned to understand each other better, to take into account each other's concerns, and to search for solutions."

Thus, in Gorbachev's view, the atmosphere of Soviet-American relations has been "improving," and both sides have been working "to make it a constant" in official contacts and in the day-to-day management of relations. Because of this improved atmosphere, as manifested by the successful summit meetings in Washington and Moscow and the agreements reached by both sides, the peoples of both nations "now have more opportunities for communication and for getting to know each other." Gorbachev was convinced that the exchange of their peoples in all professions and walks of life "will continue to enlarge and add new colors to the fabric of cooperative and even friendly relations."

The General Secretary closed with a pledge to "bequeath a safe and humane world" to future generations. To achieve this goal requires working towards it and "by working together."[135]

c.   Reagan's Remarks: A Victory for "Candor and Realism"

With a voice "frazzled with fatigue," according to one account,[136] President Reagan addressed this official audience in a spirit of gratitude for Soviet cooperation in achieving this goal and hopeful expectations of success in concluding START. At the outset the President said this ceremony is an "historic" moment. Success "has not been easy," he said, acknowledging that the General Secretary's "personal intervention was needed and proved decisive." And "for this we are grateful."

Putting the treaty in historical perspective, the President went on to say that it represented an important achievement in arms reduction whose origin was in his proposal seven years ago for a double-zero treaty. Though criticized at the time for being "unrealistic," "irresponsible," and the proposal being a "propaganda ploy" and a "geopolitical gambit," this concept has been realized in the form of the INF Treaty. On the table before them, the President continued, "we see the fruits of hope—evidence of what candor and realism can accomplish." "We have dared to hope," the President declared with a touch of theatricism, "and we have been rewarded."

President Reagan proceeded to underscore such important parts of the treaty as its elimination of an entire class of nuclear missiles for the first time; the "most stringent verification in history"; and making possible "a new dimension of cooperation between us." Even so, the President went on, "much remains on our agenda," and he cautioned Gorbachev, "We must not stop here, Mr. General Secretary; there is much more to be done."

What the President had in mind was the completion of the START treaty "as soon as possible." He urged that they "expand the frontiers of trust, even as we verify." Important "fundamental differences" remain, he went on, but the President implored that they work to narrow these differences, produce what he hoped will be "a new era of peace and expanded human freedom," and fulfill "our solemn responsibility to take steps now to reduce the chances of conflict and to prevent war." Ratification of the INF Treaty is a "first step toward a bright future, a safer world."

The President concluded with a reference to America's Western allies, giving assurances that they were fully consulted during the negotiations, that their security or their interests were not at risk, and that the treaty, indeed, enhanced their security. He also thanked the Senate for its work on the treaty, using this formal occasion televised to the Soviet people to highlight its value in the democratic process – another civic lesson. "The way of democracy is sometimes a complicated way and sometimes trying," he said, alluding to the last-minute rush to push the treaty through the Senate's ratification process, "but it is a good way, and we believe the best way."

The President's last word was for the General Secretary and the treaty negotiators. He extended his "warmest personal thanks" to Gorbachev and all those "who labored so hard for this moment."[137]

2. Joint Statement, June 1: A Summing Up of the Moscow Summit

a. Overall Appraisal of Relations

On June 1, the Soviet Union and the United States issued a joint statement of some 8,500 words summarizing the achievements of the Moscow Summit and laying out an agenda for negotiations in the immediate future. The statement was reduced to categories paralleling the agenda adopted at the Geneva Summit of 1985; namely, arms control, human rights and humanitarian concerns, regional issues, and bilateral issues.[138]

According to the joint statement, the General Secretary and the President viewed the Moscow meeting as "an important step in the process of putting U.S.-Soviet relations on a more productive and sustainable basis." Discussions took place "in a constructive atmosphere" which provided "ample opportunity for candid exchange." Hence, both sides achieved "a better understanding of each other's positions." Both leaders welcomed "the progress achieved in various areas of U.S.-Soviet relations" since their last meeting, notwithstanding "the difficulty and complexity of the issues." They also noted "with satisfaction" the numerous "concrete agreements" achieved; expressed their determination to "redouble efforts" in the months ahead where work remains to be done; and praised the "creative and intensive efforts" of the negotiators in resolving outstanding differences.[139]

b.   Dispute over "Peaceful Coexistence"

Preparation of the joint statement was not without tension and discord. A dispute arose over the next paragraph of the statement relating to the concept of "peaceful coexistence" as an essential principle in the relationship. Soviet negotiators tried but failed to persuade the U.S. side to approve of a declaration endorsing "peaceful coexistence" and renouncing the use of force to resolve disputes. Gorbachev had handed the proposed statement to the President during their first meeting on Sunday, May 29, without advance notice. "I liked the whole tone of it," the President said on June 1, but he added that his advisers found "certain ambiguities" that made the proposed formulation unacceptable.

Secretary of State Shultz reacted negatively to the proposed declaration. One unnamed U.S. official said it was "ambiguous, freighted with the baggage of the past," and, in the words of the press account, "too close for comfort to Soviet-American principles of relations negotiated in the early 1970s that collapsed with the demise of what was called then an era of detente." The official also complained that "peaceful coexistence" was a propagandistic Soviet term highlighted in their pronouncements during the 1950s and 1960s. It was, moreover, reportedly feared that reference to ruling out resolving problems "by military means" might undercut U.S. military budgets, and accepting the provision for "noninterference in internal affairs" might undercut U.S. appeals for improvements in the Soviet human rights record.

Accordingly, a "watered-down" statement was composed by senior diplomats from both sides on Monday night, going no farther than saying that the expanding U.S.-Soviet dialogue is "an increasingly effective means" of resolving disputes.[140]

c.   Arms Control Issues

Turning to arms control issues, the joint statement reiterated the commitment of both countries "to build on progress to date in arms control," to proceed towards "determined objectives and next steps on a wide range of issues," and to work "toward equitable, verifiable agreements that strengthen international stability and security."

The statement:

• acknowledged the entry of the INF Treaty into force;

- recorded in some detail the technical progress made in the joint draft text of the treaty on reducing and limiting strategic offensive arms;
- noted the signing of the agreement on notifying launches of ICBMs and SLBMs as "a practical new step, reflecting the desire...to reduce the risk of outbreak of nuclear war...";
- reaffirmed the commitment to conduct "a single forum full-scale, stage-by-stage negotiations on the issues relating to nuclear testing";
- reaffirmed the conviction of both sides that universal adherence to the Nuclear Nonproliferation Treaty was important to international peace and security and expressed the hope that other states would join in "to forego acquisition of nuclear weapons and prevent nuclear weapons proliferation";
- expressed satisfaction over the activation of the new communications link between the Nuclear Risk Reduction Center in Moscow and Washington and agreed that the centers "can play an important role:" in a future treaty reducing Soviet and American strategic nuclear arms;
- reviewed the status of ongoing multilateral negotiations and bilateral Soviet-American consultations toward a "comprehensive, effectively verifiable, and truly global ban on chemical weapons";
- emphasized the importance of "strengthening stability and security in the whole of Europe" and welcomed "progress to date on development of a mandate for new negotiations on armed forces and conventional armaments";
- expressed the hope for "an early and balanced conclusion" to the Vienna CSCE followup meeting, noting that the full implementation of the document agreed to at the Stockholm Conference "can significantly increase openness and mutual confidence"; and finally,
- reaffirmed their commitment to the further development of the CSCE process, bringing the Vienna CSCE follow-up meeting "to a successful conclusion through significant results in all the principal areas of the Helsinki Final Act and Madrid concluding document."[141]

d. Human Rights and Humanitarian Concerns

According to the joint statement, the General Secretary and the President engaged "in a detailed discussion of human rights and humanitarian concerns." They reviewed the "increasingly broad and detailed" Soviet-American dialogue in this area and agreed that "it should be conducted at all levels in order to achieve sustained, concrete progress."

The leaders also noted that this dialogue should seek "to maximize assurance of the rights, freedoms, and human dignity of individuals; promotion of people-to-people communications and contacts; active sharing of

spiritual, cultural, historical, and other values; and greater mutual understanding and respect between both countries."

To achieve these purposes, they discussed the possibility of establishing
a forum which, through regular meetings, "would bring together participants
from across the range of their two societies." They acknowledged that steps
were already being taken to establish the exchange of information and establish contacts between legislative bodies of both countries in addition to
holding discussions between persons from a wide-range of professions
directly involved in human rights matters and between representatives of
non-governmental organizations.[142]

e.   Bilateral Relations

In bilateral affairs, according to the joint statement, the General Secretary
and the President reviewed progress "in further expanding bilateral contacts, exchanges, and cooperation" since the Washington Summit in December 1987. Both leaders noted the "increasingly important role that mutually
beneficial interchange" between both countries "can play in improving
mutual understanding and providing stability" in the relationship. Both intended "to intensify such ties."

The two leaders welcomed the conclusion of a number of bilateral agreements which opened up new opportunities for "fruitful cooperation" in such
fields as: cooperation in transportation science and technology; maritime
search and rescue; operational coordination between U.S. and Soviet radio
navigation systems in the Northern Pacific and Bering Sea; and mutual
fisheries relations.

In addition, Gorbachev and Reagan,

- welcomed the recent signing and later extension of a new Memorandum
  on Civilian Nuclear Reactor Safety under the bilateral agreement on the
  Peaceful Uses of Atomic Energy;
- reviewed the status of negotiations on maritime shipping, Soviet-
  American maritime boundary, basic scientific research, emergency pollution cleanup in the Bering and Chukchi Seas;
- welcomed the start of bilateral discussions on combatting narcotics traf-
  ficking;
- welcomed the signing of a new implementing program for 1989–91 on
  the expansion of exchanges in the areas of education, science, culture,
  and sport under the general exchanges agreement; and,

- expressed satisfaction with the significant increases in people-to-people contacts and exchanges between nongovernmental organizations as "one of the most dynamic elements in the bilateral relationship."

The General Secretary and the President also took note of the "successful expansion" of scientific cooperation within the framework of bilateral agreements in environment protection, medical science and public health, artificial heart research and development, agriculture, and studies of the world oceans. They expressed "their intention to continue to expand activities under these agreements." Other areas of fruitful cooperation were acknowledged. Finally, the two sides "reconfirmed their strong support for the expansion of mutually beneficial trade and economic relations and took note of recent activity in this area. They also reaffirmed their agreement to open Consulates General in Kiev and New York as soon as practicable.

f.   Future Meetings

With respect to future meetings, the joint statement noted that the two leaders, "recognizing the importance of their personal involvement in the development of relations in the months ahead," instructed Foreign Minister Shevardnadze and Secretary Shultz to meet "as necessary and to report to them on ways to ensure continued practical progress across the full range of issues." Contacts at the expert level were also to continue "on an intensified basis."[143]

g.   Importance of Joint Statements

In conference diplomacy, as in diplomacy in general, joint statements or communiques, as they are often termed, such as this one released at the end of the Moscow Summit, are essential for making an official public record of what took place. For the Soviets, who are by political culture "document-oriented," such official statements are not only important but essential. In general, communiques or joint statements attempt to distill the essence of the conference and present documentary evidence through a summary of the proceedings of what had taken place, what had been accomplished and what remains on the agenda. They tend to accent positive gains and gloss over differences, especially when both sides, as is now the case in Soviet-American relations, wish to demonstrate "progress" in the improvement of their relationship.

Thus such joint statements as this one can at best be only a dim and fragmented reflection of the conference reality. Still, they serve a useful purpose as a "public record," despite their imperfections.

3.   Gorbachev and Reagan Press Conferences

a.   Gorbachev Praises Summit but Registers Complaints

The joint statement had to be an agreed statement. Protocol requires unanimity in such matters. This was especially true of the Moscow Summit. But it was not true of the separate press conferences held on the last day where both Gorbachev and Reagan placed their own construction on the proceedings. Gorbachev praised the achievements of the meeting, but he used the occasion to register complaints that the President had not taken advantage of an important opportunity to further improve Soviet-American relations. The General Secretary spoke candidly of "missed opportunities."

Flanked by Shevardnadze and Central Committee Secretary Anatoliy Dobrynin along with other Soviet officials, Gorbachev held his press conference at the press center of the Ministry of Foreign Affairs. It was carried live over Soviet television. Gorbachev gave an hour-long summary of the summit and responded to questions for 50 minutes. According to one report, he "appeared to be giving a careful account of what he had been able to achieve and what his efforts failed to obtain." Presumably in anticipation of the upcoming Party Conference in late June, he sought to justify his conduct at the summit and his policy of improved relations with the Reagan Administration.[144]

In his review of the summit, Gorbachev praised its achievements but complained about "missed opportunities." "The major result" of the conference, he said, "is a continuation of dialogue, which now encompasses all of the key issues of world politics, of bilateral relations." The Moscow Summit "once again, demonstrated the fact that we are indulging in a realistic dialogue." By this mutual recognition of what he called "realism in politics" that is evident in the final document, "we are laying down prerequisites, the bricks, so to say, for the building of our future relationship. It is a sign of movement into the 21st century." Gorbachev called particular attention to the success of the INF Treaty as "a common victory for reason and realism" for the benefit of both nations and all mankind.[145] In brief, the summit was to Gorbachev a "major event" that moved relations "maybe one rung or two up the ladder."[146] It was a triumph for political dialogue in creating a harmony of political interests.

Nonetheless, the General Secretary expressed what was described as "frustration and occasional exasperation" with the President and his senior advisers who accompanied him.[147] And he proceeded to vent his anger registering a number of complaints. The dispute over the inclusion of the term "peaceful coexistence" was especially annoying to Gorbachev who made his case at the last working session with the President and again publicly at the press conference. "I think we missed a chance to take an important step forward toward a civilized relationship," he said in expressing his disappointment. "It would have been a very important political signpost."[148]

Gorbachev was especially annoyed at the President's insistence on voicing and publicly demonstrating his views on human rights. During the visit, which included meetings with dissidents and religious activists, "propaganda gambits prevailed, and all sorts of spectacles," Gorbachev said, in obvious irritation. "I'm not delighted with this part of the meeting," the much annoyed Gorbachev added.[149] In defense of the Soviet view on human rights, the General Secretary explained:

> The more I think over this situation, the more I come to the conclusion that I can see that the American Administration does not have a real understanding of the real situation insofar as human rights are concerned. They must don't know about the processes in the sphere of democracy and democratization in this country.[150]

Gorbachev complained bitterly about the continuation of attacks on Soviet soldiers as they were withdrawing from Afghanistan. He blamed Pakistan for violating the Geneva accord that set forth the terms of the Soviet withdrawal. "If such attacks continue," he warned, "we shall react and react appropriately," suggesting that Soviet forces may stay in combat if fired upon.[151]

Gorbachev also complained about the failure of any positive U.S. response to Soviet proposals for a reduction of conventional arms in Europe, and he criticized U.S. officials involved in negotiations on cutting strategic offensive weapons by 50 percent. He accused them of being involved in "incomprehensible maneuvers and attempts to deviate from that issue."[152]

Furthermore, Gorbachev complained about misunderstandings on trade and economic relations, a subject on which he said there was "a very intense discussion." "Why should the dead hold onto the coattails of the living?" he asked the President, referring to the Jackson-Vanik Amendment that linked trade to Soviet fulfillment of human rights obligations. "One of them's already physically dead," he said. "The other's politically dead." And he asked rhetorically, "Why should they hang onto our coattails?" Things have changed since that amendment was passed, he emphasized in a tone of impatience, adding, "in this changed world of ours, we should think and base our policies on present-day realities."[153]

As if to sum up his catalogue of complaints about the "missed opportunities" at the Moscow Summit, Gorbachev asked the audience to share with him "one general impression":

I would not be honest with you or truthful, if I omitted to say this: It is my impression...there is a lot of contradictions in the American position.... Now, let me explain where I see this contrariness. On the one hand, we have a joint statement that there should be no war, that war is inadmissible, we are engaged in a businesslike dialogue about arms reductions, we're talking about preferences for political solutions. And yet, on the other hand, we keep hearing...we heard words about a stake made on strength.[154]

b.   Reagan Reviews the Summit: Accenting the Positive,
      the Optimistic, the Benign

After the ceremony at Vladimir Hall, the President returned to Spaso House where he had a scheduled press conference at 4:00 o'clock in the afternoon, three hours after Gorbachev's. In contrast to Gorbachev's two-hour virtuoso performance, the President's press conference lasted only 35–40 minutes. He read a brief statement and responded to questions in a hoarse voice that cracked several times. Optimistic in tone, warm and respectful of his host and the Soviet people, but flavored with realism, the President avoided hard details on the issues and tended to express himself in generalities and in his anecdotal style.[155]

As the polite guest, the President began by expressing his gratitude to the General Secretary, all his associates in the government and the people of Moscow "for all they've done to make our stay here a pleasant one and this summit conference the success it has been." A "good deal of important work," he said, has been accomplished in Moscow, and his relationship with the General Secretary and that between various members of the Soviet and American delegations "has continued to deepen and improve."

Personal relationships are not enough, the President cautioned, but he believed, nonetheless, that history would note that the U.S. approach to the summit process was one of seeking "consistency of expression as well as purpose." For his part, he confided, at every turn he had tried to state "our overwhelming desire for peace," yet at the same time realistically "to note the existence of fundamental differences." For him it was a "source of great satisfaction" that those differences "continue to recede" because of the summit meetings. The President called attention to the mutual awareness of the change in Soviet policy and government. In noting the remaining differences between both countries, the President explained: "My desire has not been to sound a note of discouragement but one of realism, not to conduct a tutorial but to give the kind of emphatic testimony to the truth that, over the long run, removes illusion and moves the process of negotiation forward."

From the American perspective, this positive and realistic approach "has borne fruit at previous meetings and at this summit conference." Referring to their first summit at Geneva, the President affirmed certain fundamental realities that would govern the relationship; namely,

> that a nuclear war cannot be won and must never be fought, that the United States and the Soviet Union bear special responsibilities for avoiding the risk of war, that neither side should seek military superiority over the other. We affirmed our determination to prevent war, whether nuclear or conventional, and our resolve to contribute in every way possible, along with other nations, to a safer world.

Both leaders had established a "broad agenda and initiated a new process of dialogue" at Geneva to address tensions in the relationship. Since that time, the President declared, "we have achieved through a sustained effort progress across this broad agenda." And then he cited the first item on his agenda, human rights, because this matter is "fundamental" to relations with Moscow and with other nations of the world. He confided to never having failed to make this point from the beginning and was now "encouraged by recent signs of progress in the Soviet Union" as the weight of totalitarian rule has been somewhat eased.

Since the Geneva meeting both he and Gorbachev, the President continued, "have worked to build a relationship of greater trust." To do this they sought to improve understanding between the two countries through broader people-to-people contacts. As a result, agreements have been concluded to expand a wide range of bilateral cooperation. On regional issues, discussed in full, progress was evident in the Soviet decision to withdraw from Afghanistan and the mutual pledge to reach peaceful solutions to regional conflicts. The exchange of INF ratification instruments symbolized steady progress with each summit meeting to achieve the goal of reducing each nation's strategic arsenals. "Important additional strides" toward verification have been made, a matter "most important" and one of the "more difficult issues for us." Progress was made in other areas and here he cited agreements reached at Moscow on an experiment to improve the verification of existing nuclear treaties and notification of strategic ballistic missile launches.

The President concluded his formal statement saying "how deeply moving" he found his discussions with the various citizens of the Soviet Union. As if to highlight the importance of these encounters and of progress towards his goals in human rights, the President concluded:

> The monks of Danilov, the dissidents and refuseniks, the writers and artists, the students and young people have shown once again that

spiritual values are cherished in this nation. It's my fervent hope that those values will attain even fuller expression.

Having finished his formal statement, the President invited questions from the journalists. Among the points raised by reporters and responded to (sometimes obliquely) by the President were the following:

- On matters requiring trust and determining whether the Cold War has ended, the relationship is based first and foremost on the principle "trust but verify." The "very productive meetings" at Moscow from the perspective of both sides suggest a favorable "atmosphere now."
- Differences continue on the "infinitely more complex START Treaty (compared with the less complex INF Treaty); negotiations on a number of point are going forward, the details of which he purposely avoided; those differences were expected to be eliminated during the remainder of his Administration or that of his successor's, but without setting any deadlines which he abhorred.
- "I am dead set against deadlines" that affect time but not substance.
- Progress has been made towards improving human rights in the Soviet Union, citing as an example the fact that 300 people have been freed from imprisonment and restrictions have been eased on emigration.
- Positive change in the Soviet Union has been due to Gorbachev, particularly a willingness to negotiate allowing sufficient progress so that "we can look with optimism on future negotiations."
- In contrast to Gorbachev's view expressed at his press conference arguing that SDI was a means for achieving superiority in space, the Administration's view was that SDI would "make it virtually impossible for nuclear missiles to get through to their targets in another country," hence providing the instrument for "total elimination" of nuclear weapons and creating "a lot better world."
- Both sides are "coming to a point" of reducing conventional weapons along the European front and conventional forces as well as nuclear forces. But the "simple removing of a half a million men [as Gorbachev proposed at their first session] would not exactly equal because his military would be moved a short distance back away from the front."
- Neither Gorbachev nor any others among the leadership had voiced objections to meetings with dissidents and remarks at Danilov Monastery and before the writer's union but he had "a feeling that in some way our concern with this" was "interfering" in "internal government policies." Americans perceive as "very much our business to bring" an injustice to the attention of the government.

- "Peaceful coexistence" appeared to have a mutually acceptable "tone," but "ambiguities" existed requiring that despite "agreement with the general thought," some "rewriting was done by our own people."
- Bureaucracies once created have a "fundamental rule above all others — preserve the bureaucracy," and, therefore, the reference to the Soviet bureaucracy's blame for the Soviet emigration problem in the speech at Moscow University was a reference to his general perception of any bureaucracy which may have had "a possibility" of application in the case of Soviet restricted emigration (implying that Gorbachev may not have been directly responsible).
- On what he learned on his first trip to Moscow: "I think that one of the most wonderful forces for stability and good that I have seen in the Soviet Union are the Russian women."

c.   Making Points to the World Media

The press conference freed Gorbachev and Reagan from the binding formality of the joint statement and enabled them to freely make their own assessment of the Moscow Summit to the world media.

Clearly, Gorbachev had more to clarify than Reagan. He did this by registering serious complaints that invoked criticism of the U.S. side and suggested deeper failures of the conference. Accordingly, he publicly chastised the President for reneging on his initial approval of the Soviet formula for the term "peaceful coexistence"; criticized his "misperception" of human rights in the Soviet Union; threatened to halt withdrawal of Soviets troops from Afghanistan if the attacks by the Pakistani-supported Mujahedin guerrilla fighters continue; sharply reproved the American side for failing to address the reduction of conventional arms in Europe and for their continued adherence to SDI and the loose interpretation of the ABM Treaty that prevented progress in reducing strategic weapons by 50 percent; and ridiculed continued U.S. adherence to trade restrictions in Jackson-Vanik. Gorbachev thus made his critical points. But he also balanced his criticism somewhat with a positive appraisal of the summit as a whole, particularly the completion of the INF Treaty as a milestone in arms control, and a reaffirmation of the Soviet commitment to dialogue.

In contrast, the President continued to follow his overall strategy of benign restraint and "friendly persuasion," taking the high road in his appraisal of the meeting. He reiterated his known positions on human rights and strategic weapons, while praising progress made in other areas of arms control negotiations, acknowledging approvingly progress in Gorbachev's reform program, and showing his deep respect for the Soviet people, especially Soviet women. Most importantly, the President, like the General Secretary, reaffirmed his commitment to a continuing superpower dialogue.

4.   Socializing in the Evening

Early in the evening the General Secretary, the President and their wives attended a special ballet performance at the Bolshoi Theater. Leading ballet dancers of the Bolshoi performed seven scenes to music by Tchaikovsky, Glazunov, Khachaturian, Shostakovich and Drigo. Despite the tension generated in the press conferences, both leaders were described as being "in good humor" as they sat in the royal box in this 19th Century neo-classical theater, decorated with Soviet and American national flags, listened to the orchestra play the national anthems of both countries and watched the ballet performance.[156]

After the ballet, the General Secretary, the President and their wives drove to an official guest residence in the northwestern outskirts of Moscow for a private supper. After supper, the Reagans returned to Spaso House, stopping briefly along the say for a stroll around the flood-lit Red Square shortly before midnight. Walking hand-in-hand the Reagans were cheered by hundreds of onlookers. "We are here because Nancy had not seen it, and we're leaving tomorrow and I didn't want her to miss it," the President said as they stood below the multi-colored domes of St. Basil's Cathedral.[157]

So ended the fourth day of the Moscow Summit.

5.   The Moscow Summit: A Congealing of Essential Elements

By the end of the fourth day, the last day of formal negotiations, the character of the Moscow Summit had been firmly set — the essential elements had congealed. Unlike the get-acquainted and agenda-setting Geneva Summit of 1985, the high-rolling, almost "go-for-broke" negotiations at the Reykjavik Summit of 1986 that ended in an arms control deadlock, and the Washington Summit of 1987 with its successful completion of the INF Treaty, the Moscow Summit was as much a celebration of past accomplishments as a forum for grappling with the future.[158]

The formal tone and essence of the joint statement officially proclaimed the achievements of the past three years and affirmed the negotiating agenda for the remainder of the Reagan Administration, and possibly its successor. The press conferences revealed the inner frustrations of a Soviet leader whose domestic agenda fueled a quickening pace for successful arms control negotiations and the stolid determination of a President who though outwardly congenial and seemingly accommodating was not prepared to concede a defense concept that he believed vital and that many observers believed was largely responsible for bringing the Soviets to the negotiating table; namely, SDI.

Thus it was with mixed feelings of success, frustration and certitude bred of adhering inflexibly to an uncompromising belief that both leaders bade their farewells.

E. FINAL DAY AND REAGAN'S DEPARTURE, THURSDAY AND FRIDAY, JUNE 2–3

1. Bidding Farewell at St. George's Hall

a. Gorbachev's Remarks: Gratitude, Optimism with Note of Urgency for the Future

The General Secretary and the President ended their Moscow Summit where it had begun, at a farewell meeting under the glittering chandeliers and vaulted ceiling of the elegant St. George's Hall in the Kremlin. Both were accompanied by their wives and members of the official party. Gorbachev spoke first, expressing gratitude for the success of their meeting, optimism for what the successful completion of what remains to be done, and a note of urgency in quickening the pace of future negotiations and accommodation of interests.

The General Secretary thanked the President and his colleagues "for cooperation, openness, and a businesslike approach" to their negotiations at this Moscow Summit. Both sides have "every reason" to consider the meeting and the President's visit "a useful contribution to the development of dialogue between the Soviet Union and the United States."

Gorbachev noted that he and the President have been "dealing with each other" for three years. "From the first exchange of letters to the conclusion of this meeting," he continued in a tone of satisfaction, "we've come a long way." However, the General Secretary acknowledged frankly that, "Our dialogue has not been easy," adding with some feeling, using the metaphor of a train on a track, "we mustered enough realism and political will to overcome obstacles and divert the train of Soviet-U.S. relations from a dangerous track to a safer one." Yet he added this tactfully stated criticism more forcefully expressed in his press conference: "It has, however, so far been moving much more slowly than is required by the real situation, both in our two countries and in the whole world."

Expressing his understanding that the President was "willing to continue our joint endeavors," the General Secretary, speaking for the Soviet side, pledged that "we will do everything in our power to go on moving forward." Supported by the "vast experience" gained at the previous summits and "backed up by their achievements," both nations "are in duty, bound to dis-

play still greater determination and consistency." Such were the expectations of both the Soviet and American peoples, international public opinion
and the entire world community.

In conclusion, the General Secretary asked the President to convey to the
American people the best wishes of the Soviet people and somewhat poeti-
cally reiterated his pledge of "peaceful coexistence": "Over the past 3 years,
our two nations have come to know each other better. They have now taken
a really good look at each other's eyes and have a keener sense of the need
to live together on this beautiful planet."[159]

b.   Reagan's Remarks: Gratitude, Appreciation and a Sense of Humanity

In what was described as "a remarkably emotional" farewell speech,
President Reagan left no doubt of his satisfaction with the Moscow Summit.
Flanked by Nancy Reagan, Gorbachev and his wife, Raisa, the President
gave clear evidence of being "deeply moved" by his four days of summit
negotiations and intimate interaction with some of the Soviet people, a nation whose Communist leadership he used to criticize harshly.[160]

The President began by frankly admitting that "this is an emotional moment" for him and Mrs. Reagan. Both had been "truly moved by the warmth
and the generous hospitality" received from "all of our Soviet hosts...but
most especially, from the two of you," referring to the Gorbachevs. The
President acknowledged that he "appreciated and valued" the exchanges
that had taken place and the "long hours of hard work that we and our experts put in to make progress on the difficult issues we face." This brief visit
also allowed them, he continued, "to know, if only briefly, your art treasures
and your people: artists, writers, individuals from all walks of life — people
who were willing to share with us their experiences, their fears, their hopes."

Alluding to the hall where this summit began and was now ending, the
President observed that it was named for the Order of St. George, and then
proceeded, revealing his intuitive understanding of the theatrical moment,
to make this warm and moving statement flavored with religious feeling and
mixed with political expectations:

> I would like to think our efforts during these past days have slayed a
> few dragons and advanced the struggle against the evils that threaten
> mankind — threats to peace and liberty. And I would like to hope that,
> like St. George, with God's help, peace and freedom can prevail.

Adding a personal note, the President recalled telling the young people
at Moscow State University that they appeared in his eyes "exactly as would
any group of students "in the United States or anywhere else in the world.

Similarly, both he and Mrs. Reagan found "the faces, young and old, here on the streets of Moscow." At first, they were "curious faces," but as time went on, "the smiles began and then the waves." Such expressions of friendship and affection were reciprocated with equal vigor.

In conclusion, the President again expressed his gratitude to the Gorbachevs for their friendship and hospitality and wanted them "to know we think" of them "as friends." "In that spirit," he asked the General Secretary one further favor. He proceeded to make this somewhat sentimental appeal that reflected the human dimension of the summit that he had sought to emphasize:

> Tell the people of the Soviet Union of the deep feelings of friendship felt by us and by the people of our country toward them. Tell them, too, Nancy and I are grateful for their coming out to see us, grateful for their waves and smiles, and tell them we will remember all of our days, their faces — the faces of hope — hope for a new era in human history, an era of peace between our nations and our peoples.[161]

c. Departure from Moscow

The President's farewell remarks left two impressions: one that he strongly endorsed the favorable mood generated by Soviet-American cooperation that prevailed during the summit negotiations; and the other, that his remarks had highlighted the warmth that gradually built up between the President and the Soviet citizenry during his brief stay in Moscow. At first curious about the visiting U.S. President, Soviet crowds initially gathered mostly to capture a glimpse of him climbing in and out of his limousine. But as the Reagans motored out of the Kremlin towards the Vnukovo Airport for a departure flight to London, the Soviet people, who had clearly been following the visit with interest through the Soviet media, especially the television, lined the streets and broke into a steady applause.[162]

As in the case of the President's arrival, an honor guard was mustered at the airport. National flags of the Soviet Union and the United States were hoisted on tall flagstaffs. As the President, his wife and the official party drove up to the airport building and stepped on to the tarmac, the band struck up the national anthems of both countries. And according to formal protocol on such occasions, President Gromyko and President Reagan inspected the honor guard made up of the three Soviet Armed forces: the Army, the Air Force and the Navy.

After the formal inspection, the honor guard marched off as the band played martial music. Final handshakes at the ramp by Gromyko and his wife, Shevarnadze and Dobrynin concluded the ceremony as the President and Mrs. Reagan boarded the airliner for the stopover flight to London.[163]

2.   Stopover in London and Address at Guildhall

The Presidential party arrived in London on the same day, Thursday, June 2. The President and Mrs. Reagan had tea with Queen Elizabeth II at Buckingham Palace. Later in the day, the President and his senior aides briefed Prime Minister Margaret Thatcher at 10 Downing Street on the summit. Secretary Shultz had flown to NATO headquarters in Brussels where he briefed the Allied foreign ministers and other representatives. An aide to Mrs. Thatcher said that she "strongly supported" the President's "approach to human rights and his raising it the way he did [at the summit]." The Prime Minister was also satisfied that the United States would not rush into completing a treaty on offensive strategic weapons.[164]

On June 3, the next day, the President, appearing relaxed and rested and not at all visibly fatigued as he was half way through the Moscow Summit, addressed the Royal Institute of International Affairs at the 15th Century Guildhall in London.[165] With Prime Minister Thatcher looking on approvingly, the President celebrated the Moscow Summit as marking a "turning point" in East-West relations and said that "a worldwide movement toward democracy" was ushering in "the hope of a new era in human history, and, hopefully an era of peace and freedom for all." The President reported that Gorbachev "is a serious man, seeking serious reform," and expressed his belief that "democratic reform" initiated by the General Secretary was making progress and accordingly deserved the encouragement and prayers of the West. "Quite possibly," the President said, "we are entering an era of history, a time of lasting change in the Soviet Union," but he added cautiously, "We will have to see." Other cautionary notes were sounded despite what was described as the President's "glowing appraisal." He noted that the West must remain militarily strong and be unafraid to engage the Soviets in a spirit of "realism and public candor" which he termed "the best way to avoid war or conflict."

Addressing the issue of human rights, the President declared that if free nations "question their own faith in freedom" and do not speak out against human rights abuses, "they cease telling the truth to themselves." According to one observer, the President's references to human rights had "strong religious overtones." At one point the President entoned, "I pray that the hand of the Lord will be on the Soviet people...." And at another he quoted from Isaiah and presented what he called "our formula for completing our crusade for freedom." "Our faith is in a higher law," he said, adding with feeling, "Yes, we believe in prayer and its power. And like the founding fathers of both our lands, we hold that humanity was meant not to be dishonored by the all-powerful state but to live in the image and likeness of Him who made us."

The President concluded with references to the wartime friendship between President Franklin D. Roosevelt and Prime Minister Winston Churchill, alluding to that friendship as a symbol of the close ties between the United States and Britain and his own friendship with Mrs. Thatcher. "Come, my friends, as it was said of old by Tennyson," the President implored, "It is not too late to seek a newer world."

Before leaving London, the President conferred with Japanese Prime Minister Noboru Takeshita at Winfield House, the U.S. Ambassador's residence. Posing for photographers with Takeshita, the President answered questions from the press and once again reiterated his support for Gorbachev's reform goals. The Soviet leader "very definitely" intends to proceed with perestroika and glasnost, the President said, "and it's a definite improvement in the way things are done."[166]

3. Arrival in Washington

a. Reception at Andrews Air Force Base

At 4:35 p.m. June 3, the President's plane landed at Andrews Air Force Base. There he was met by Vice President George Bush, the entire Cabinet, an honor guard, a 21-gun salute and a partisan crowd of nearly 4,000 that waved welcoming signs one of which read: "You've tamed the Evil Empire."[167]

b. Report on Achievements at Moscow

In a speech marked with high emotion and deeply patriotic references along with a reiteration of basic American democratic principles, the President reported on his meeting with General Secretary Gorbachev. Assuring his audience with the old American saying that, "there's no place like home," the President alluded to George M. Cohan to affirm the propriety of "all this red, white, and blue scenery" that "some may call...flag waving," but right now, to "two weary travelers'" he said, "I can't think of a better flag to wave."

A "little tired" but "exhilarated at what has happened" and "exhilarated, too, at the thought of the future and what may lie ahead for young people of America and all of the world," the President described his week in Moscow as "momentous—not conclusive perhaps, but momentous." But "right now momentous will do just fine." Expressing a unity of belief among Americans on the principles of peace and freedom, the President said that "peace and freedom are what this trip was about." Some "real progress" was achieved in several areas in Moscow—on human rights, regional conflicts, an expansion of personal contacts, concluding the INF ratification exchanges, and "tangible progress" toward achieving a 50 percent reduction of nuclear weapons. "All of this was good and promising for the future," he said.

Turning to the personal side of the visit, Reagan noted his pleasure at seeing the faces of the Soviet people, the young students at Moscow State University, hardly different from any other group of students, the faces he saw on the "streets of Moscow," repeating his earlier observation that "they were curious faces" but as time went on "the smiles began and then the waves," a reaction that was amply reciprocated by the President and the First Lady. A truth was registered once again, he said, that "It isn't people, but governments that make war. And it isn't people, but governments that erect barriers that keep us apart."

Much is changing in the Soviet Union, the President reported. "We hope and pray that the signs of change continue there." And he declared that both he and Gorbachev have pledged "to work to continue building a better understanding between our two countries." But despite progress in relations and expected "bumps in the road," the President reminded his listeners that the anticipated positive changes were derived from the strategy that was based "on faith in the eventual triumph of human freedom." It was this conviction that "defines us as a people and a nation." Even veteran journalists were tearfully moved by the sight they never thought would take place in their lifetime:

> an American President there in the heart of Moscow talking about economic, political, and individual freedoms to the future leaders of the Soviet Union; explaining that freedom makes a difference, and explaining how freedom works; talking, too, about the possibility of a new age of prosperity and peace, where old antagonisms between nations can someday be put behind us, a new age that can be ours if only we'll reach out to it.

The President went on to speak of a "sudden, startling future" that may be before the young people, a future brought on by a technological and information revolution based on understanding the "nexus between economic growth and creative freedom." But the President hoped that young Americans, indeed all Americans, will "always remember that this revolution is only the continuation of a revolution begun two centuries ago, a revolution of hope...that someday a new land might become a place where freedom's light would beacon forth." Now "more than ever," the President declared, "we must continue" the selfless dedication to the principles of freedom. To falter or fail would be to invite the "harsh" judgment of future generations upon us. In an allusion to an intensely patriotic theme familiar to the American tradition as it emerged in the 18th and 19th Centuries the President pleaded:

> Let us resolve to continue, one nation, one people, united in our love of peace and freedom, determined to keep our defenses strong, to stand with those who struggle for freedom across the world, to keep America a shining city, a light unto the nations.

Yet the President sternly reminded his listeners that "there's work remaining here at home," and cautioned that whatever success we have achieved, "we must never be prideful toward others." Americans have much to learn from other peoples and cultures; they should never "grow content." Nor should they rest "until every American of every race or background knows the full blessing of liberty, until justice for all is truly justice for all." In an allusion to the religious roots of America the President declared that being an American means "remembering another loyalty, a loyalty, as the hymn puts it, 'to another country I have heard of, a place whose King is never seen and whose armies cannot be counted!'"

Continuing along this religious-patriotic vein, the President recalled that "if patriotism is not the only thing, it is one of the best things," and Americans "can be grateful to God that we have seen such a rebirth of it here in this country." The President proceeded to recite this familiar verse to sustain his belief in this historic time of the Nation's history: "If tomorrow, all things were gone I'd worked for all my life, and I had to start again with just my children and my wife, I'd thank my lucky stars to be living here today cause the flag still stands for freedom and they can't take that away."

"We think our friend Lee Greenwood has it just right," the President concluded: "'All our days, and especially today, there ain't no doubt we love this land. God bless the U.S.A.'"[168]

c. Its Meaning: Affirmation of the President's Democratic Philosophy

Thus spoke the President: It is an extension of the emotions and convictions, idealism and moralism expressed in his Guildhall speech; a plea for an enduring commitment to human freedom as the essential nexus between creative political liberty and economic and technological success; recognition of dependency on a Supreme Being; an emotional statement on American patriotism, some may say more suited to the turn-of-the-20th Century religious-minded, intensely patriotic, moralistic and idealistic American than to those more secular-minded and skeptical who are about to enter the 21st Century.

Yet, it is a speech whose value seems to lie in the fact that it is the response of a President whose beliefs in the historic American tradition run deep, whose past views of the "Evil Empire" had been unrestrainedly critical, and whose views had radically changed after a brief exposure to a totalitarian Soviet system caught up in the throes of systemic change that promises greater freedom. And in this response there is confirmation of his view that change toward greater freedom offers greater possibilities for world peace and security. In brief, the President's speech like so many others delivered in Moscow is a reaffirmation of his democratic philosophy and the promise he believes it offers for mankind.

III

Results and Significant Aspects
of the Moscow Summit

A. ON THE RESULTS: LIMITED EXPECTATIONS, LIMITED GAINS

Symbolism and ceremony plus some substantive achievements best describe the characteristics and results of the Moscow Summit. At the outset Soviet and American perspectives were asymmetrical: The Soviets looked for some positive movement on their arms control agenda; the Americans expected no breakthrough in arms control and at most seemed satisfied with accruing some political benefits from the symbolism and ceremony of a summit that highlighted human rights and from progress on regional issues. In general, the expectations on both sides were limited, and so were the results.

The joint statement, summarized above, records the achievements and, by implication, the failures at Moscow. Exchange of INF Treaty ratification instruments that put the treaty into force was perhaps the most significant practical accomplishment. Beyond that the practical achievements were modest, as for example in arms control, agreement on notification of missile testing. Agreements were also reached in such functional areas as international exchanges, space cooperation, maritime search and rescue, fisheries, transportation and radio navigation. An agreement in principle emerged in discussions on regional issues, specifically with respect to the withdrawal of Cuban troops from Angola.

In post-summit commentary, White House aides acknowledged that the seven agreements concluded at Moscow, covering the functional areas noted above, had amounted to very little, giving credence to the oft-made observation that the summit was long on symbolism but short on substance.

However, they also added that this accomplishment brought to 47 the number of two-way cooperative pacts signed in the last three years, suggesting a contribution to creating a favorable climate of relations that has substantial value in diplomacy. One White House aide captured this aspect of the summit results, when he remarked with respect to these agreements: "Are they big agreements? No, they're peanuts. But that's coral-building. You're slowly building up a relationship of trust and agreements."[169]

Summit results can, therefore, be measured against initial expectations, and judgments on success or failure be made accordingly. But tangible, concrete results, such as in the signing of practical accords, are an incomplete criterion; they tell only part of the story. For summitry is political interaction at the apex of national power. Other elements enter into the equation. And it is often in this intangible, vaporous area of inter-relationships where another and perhaps more realistic and accurate measure of success or failure can be taken. Both Gorbachev and Reagan understood this when they passed their final judgments on the significance of the Moscow Summit.

B.   SIGNIFICANT ASPECTS OF THE SUMMIT

1.   Keeping the Superpower Dialogue Going

a.   Appraisals by Gorbachev and Reagan

(1) Gorbachev: A "Major Event" and "Continuation of a Dialogue." Both Gorbachev and Reagan acknowledged the limited achievements of the Moscow Summit, but the transcending significance for both was the conviction that their meeting had kept the superpower dialogue on track and moving forward.

Gorbachev was annoyed at Reagan's persistent emphasis on human rights; he complained bitterly of the "missed opportunities" in the negotiations with the President; he was visibly frustrated by the lack of movement on reducing strategic weapons; and he criticized the American side for permitting the dead hand of the past (in the form of the Jackson-Vanik Amendment) to restrict and impair economic and commercial relations. Nonetheless, for Gorbachev the Moscow Summit was a "major event" that illustrated the "importance of the dialogue" between the Soviet Union and the United States, and confirmed the validity of efforts to develop a new relationship.[170] "This meeting has shown how right we were in choosing the path we took in Geneva," Gorbachev said. "The president's visit will serve to improve Soviet-American relations."[171]

The General Secretary portrayed the principal achievements at the Moscow meeting as being the "continuation of a dialogue" that "now envelops all key problems of world policy," together with "a demonstration that this dialogue has become infused with a sense of realism" that insures its durability as a process. He regretted that "more could not have been achieved," but he tempered this negative judgment with the observation that "politics is the art of the possible." In his view the visit had also enabled the President to gain a better understanding of Soviet society, and he praised him for his "sense of realism."[172]

Recall that even before the Moscow meeting, Gorbachev had acknowledged in his interview with The Washington Post that, "The winds of the Cold War are being replaced by the winds of hope." Whether true or not, the very discussion of such possibilities by Soviet and American negotiators indicated what was described as the "sweeping transformation" that was taking place in Soviet-American relations. What the summit represented in Gorbachev's mind was, therefore, a further codification of that change. For, as Gorbachev told his Post interviewers, "the most important political result in the recent period of improvement in our relations is the regular and very productive political dialogue that we have been having." "The important thing," he added, optimistically, "is that if the dialogue continues, it will lead to specific achievements.[173]

(2) Reagan: Building a "Sustainable," "Long Term" Relationship. President Reagan valued the Moscow meeting for the opportunities it gave him to speak about the liberating properties in a broadening of human rights. But implied in his utterances was a conviction that the Moscow Summit was another step forward in a deepening and enriching dialogue between the Soviet Union and the United States. For this reason, he said on returning home, the meeting with Gorbachev had produced "a sense of hope, a powerful hope" for improvement in Soviet-American relations.[174]

The President viewed the Moscow meeting retrospectively, as another milestone in the journey that had begun in Geneva in 1985. "Impressive progress" had thus far been achieved in all areas of a common agenda, he said in his welcoming address. For him the message of the Moscow meeting about to begin was clear: "despite clear and fundamental differences, and despite the inevitable frustrations that we have encountered, our work has begun to produce results." The President expressed confidence that the "tremendous hurdles" that they faced could be overcome because, "we share a common goal: strengthening the framework we have already begun to build for a relationship that we can sustain over the long term. . . ."[175] And in his press conference at the close of the summit, the President repeated this theme of building a relationship through dialogue: "We also set a broad agenda and initiated a new process of dialogue to address the sources of tension in U.S.-Soviet relations. Since Geneva, we have achieved through a sustained effort progress across this broad agenda."[176]

Implying the value of summitry and dialogue, the President acknowledged on another occasion in Moscow that "we have established the kind of working relationship I think we both had in mind when we first met in Geneva." In the negotiating process, he continued, "We've been candid about our differences but sincere in sharing a common objective and working hard together to draw closer to it." Always searching for areas of agreement, he said, "We and our two governments have both gotten into the habit of looking for those areas. We found more than we expected."[177]

Reagan foresaw peace, security, and freedom emerging from this search for accommodation. Upon returning home, the President readily acknowledged that "seeds of freedom and greater trust were sown" during his meetings with Gorbachev. "And I just have to believe that, in ways we may not be able to guess, those seeds will take root and grow."[178]

Perhaps the President best described American expectations of a continuing dialogue in his off-hand remarks made while walking with Gorbachev through Red Square. In responding to a comment by Gorbachev that "everything is being done to ensure there is greater mutual understanding between our countries," the President said with disarming simplicity: "We decided to talk with one another and not about one another. And we are doing quite well."[179]

The Moscow Summit provided the opportunity for continuing dialogue, and when it appeared that obstacles to a START treaty would not be surmounted, discussions were reported on the possibility of holding a fifth summit, if agreement could be reached before the end of the Reagan Administration. And if this were not possible and negotiations were continuing, then the President pledged (to an amenable Gorbachev) to "do everything I can to persuade my successor to follow up and to continue. . . ."[180]

Thus both Gorbachev and Reagan placed a high value on the Moscow Summit as a forum for superpower dialogue, and these convictions were shared by aides and the media in both countries.

(3) Aides and the Media: Supporting Views. (a) *From the Soviet Side.* Glasnost had not extended to such lengths that Soviet officials would second-guess the General Secretary. Nor were American officials prepared to voice assessments in contradiction to their chief. Uniformly both sides laid special stress on the high value of the meeting at Moscow.

Moscow's "exhaustive" coverage of the summit seemed designed to emphasize the positive aspects of the meeting and thus enhance Gorbachev's domestic and international stature on the eve of the forthcoming 19th Party Conference. The Soviet leadership sought to project an image of unity behind the General Secretary's conduct of the dialogue with Reagan. This approach received authoritative expression when the Politburo "fully approved" the results of the summit, perceiving in this process a "deepening of the political dialogue" between both sides as the "principal result" of the conference. The Politburo concluded that a "constructive basis for the long-term development" of Soviet-American relations had been established. The summit was also said to have confirmed the "correctness" of Soviet policy towards the United States set by the April 1985 Central Committee plenum, based on "realism" and the "new political thinking," and carried out by Gorbachev.[181]

On June 7, a Pravda editorial authoritatively acclaimed the summit as being "an event of major international significance—that is the virtually unanimous theme of the reaction to the Moscow meeting." The editorial continued:

> The process of normalizing Soviet-U.S. relations which is now underway is of exceptional significance here. The definite improvement of these relations, symbolized by the summit meetings, make it possible to count on a fundamental move toward the elimination of the nuclear threat. . . . The Moscow meeting was not only an outstanding political event in the history of our countries' mutual relations but also a landmark in world politics. Its main result was the continuation and development of Soviet-U.S. dialogue. Furthermore, this is now a dialogue whose attention is centered on the discussion and solution of questions which vitally concern the peoples of our two countries and all mankind.[182]

Soviet commentators and foreign policy specialists in the Foreign Ministry and institutes chimed in the chorus of approval, proclaiming as if in one voice the importance of a continuing dialogue with the United States.

Yevgeniy Primakov, director of the prestigious Institute of World Economy and International Relations, seemed to speak for the entire Soviet intellectual community when in a Vremya television interview he judged the Moscow meeting to be "very significant." "The continuity of the process," he went on, "has become marked." And turning to the substance of the meeting, he added, "I would say that constructiveness. . .of the conversations is becoming richer." The frequency of the meetings has made it possible for the two leaders to deal with problems as known negotiators who have familiarity with the issues on the table. "Each time they can talk more and more freely," he said. But most importantly the positive changes in public opinion in the West, coupled with those in the Soviet Union generated by the new political thinking, have produced "not just individual, but more thoroughgoing and, objective considerations which create opportunities for a constructive exchange of views, which are becoming richer with each successive meeting."[183]

Most important was the assessment of Aleksandr A. Bessmertnykh, Soviet Deputy Foreign Minister and participant in the summit negotiations, voiced over Moscow's prestigious Studio 9 television program. Bessmertnykh discounted those assessments that stressed the failure of not having achieved more substantive agreements at Moscow. Looking at the whole chain of summits during the past three years, he observed, "none of us would say that the other three summits were in any way inferior to this one." Bessmertnykh visualized each summit as "a step forward along the path to a certain goal." Results of summits, he continued, had to be judged according to the goals established. Addressing the "problem of atmosphere," he noted, "certainly, the Moscow summit — the whole world is saying this — has brought about a certain calm into international relations as a whole." "Everyone is feeling this," he added. Secondly, at the conceptual level of analysis, the conclusions reached by both leaders at the Moscow meeting were "extraordinarily important" and include "the reality of conducting business with each other, political methods in solving questions, and dialogue as a driving force in U.S.S.R.-U.S. relations." Finally, there "is the layer of specific agreements." "Thank heaven, this time there were many...," he proclaimed enthusiastically, describing them as spanning the spectrum from the military and political areas to economic, scientific, and people-to-people relationships. Therefore, Bessmertnykh concluded:

> the total effect of the summit, its total effect on Soviet-U.S. relations and on the world situation as a whole, provides the answer to your question [regarding "the actual results — of the summit, about what yardstick should be applied in measuring the success or failure of such a meeting."] Truly, it was a giant step forward in the cause of normalizing the world situation and improving Soviet-U.S. relations — truly, a very significant event.[184]

(b) From the American Side. The President came away from Moscow "exhilarated" by what happened and, as he acknowledged, "at the thought of the future and what may lie ahead for the young people of America and the world." "The events of this week in Moscow," he said, were "momentous — not conclusive, perhaps, but momentous. And believe me, right now momentous will do just fine." In apparent justification for summitry, the President assessed the Moscow meeting as being "good and promising for the future."[185]

American officials vocally supported the President's positive assessment. Lt. Gen. Colin L. Powell, his national security adviser, expanded on the President's theme in an interview abroad Air Force One on the return home.

The superpowers have developed a "fairly stable, maturing relationship that I think will continue regardless of what the administration is," said Powell. "We cannot allow this relationship to be governed by when this administration ends and the next one begins." "We are moving beyond individual problems to a broader discussion of systemic difference," Powell said in a plea for continuity. "You don't make any sudden turns; you just let it grow at a natural pace." Powell cited expanding relations in such areas as increased student exchanges and exchanges in the professions as further signs of improvement and growing stability in the relationship. Addressing the issue of Gorbachev's proposal for a bilateral legislative seminar on human rights, Powell described it "an interesting idea" but declined to characterize it as a smoke screen to divert attention from Soviet violations of human rights. "Any opportunity we have to expand the length and breadth of our relationship is positive," he said. "We tend not to suffer from this kind of broad exchange."[186]

The national security adviser "bridled" at suggestions that the Moscow Summit was primarily pomp and circumstance with little substance and that it produced nothing that couldn't have been done before lunch by an assistant secretary of state and his Soviet counterpart. "Is there substance in the President speaking at the Danilov Monastery? To students at Moscow State University? At the House of Writers?" he asked, rhetorically. "I submit to you that there's real substance. . .that goes well beyond style and cannot be accomplished" by an assistant secretary of state, he argued with some intensity.[187]

In general, U.S. officials were pleased that the Moscow dialogue had deepened on all issues on the Soviet-American agenda: human rights, bilateral ties, regional problems and arms control. "We have institutionalized things," said Jack Matlock, U.S. Ambassador to Moscow. "So the whole balance of these issues is coming together. All four are now moving in sync, and this is what we wanted to accomplish."[188]

For all the pomp and circumstance in Moscow and the lack of major agreements, notably failure to remove the technical roadblocks to conclude a START treaty, the summit was viewed by American officials as helping to consolidate a relationship that had been moving toward greater stability and realism. As one on-the-scene U.S. correspondent put it, "It set a constructive tone that will be harder to disrupt and anchors relations such that it will be harder for the conservative right [on both sides] to attack." "The main thing," said a senior State Department official, "is that we and they are now postured in a way to do serious business with each other without being directed by domestic pressures in managing a difficult relationship." "We can now talk and express our disagreements," the official said, suggesting the growing maturity of the relationship with each summit, "and when there are raw feelings this does not break down the dialogue. That is healthy."[189]

Among editorial opinion in the major American press, the Christian Science Monitor might well have expressed a fairly common appraisal in support of the Moscow Summit. "By traditional measures," the Monitor's editors noted, the achievements at Moscow were "modest;" namely, expanded cultural exchanges; some confidence-building measures in the arms control area; and agreements on the peaceful uses of outer space, for example. "But the summit is nonetheless valuable in laying a stable foundation for future U.S.-Soviet relations and for the example it sets as an alternative to confrontation."[190]

Thus, the Moscow Summit provided another unique opportunity for accelerating the momentum of what had become institutionalized Soviet-American summitry that had begun in Geneva during November 1985. Moscow provided a forum for resolving differences through diplomacy and negotiations. It permitted political interaction at the highest level and accordingly opened up the possibility for inching ever so slowly forward in resolving major issues in dispute. Pomp and ceremony did put a high gloss on this superpower dialogue. And largely, only peripheral issues — "peanuts," as one U.S. official termed them — in the relationship were resolved in negotiated agreements. But serious business was, nonetheless, going on beneath it all. The deeper, unresolved issues in arms control that lay at the core-center of the relationship were addressed, but, ultimately, deferred for a future agenda.

b.   On the Future Agenda

(1) Deferring Unresolved Arms Control Issues. "In a broader sense," wrote Gerald F. Seib of The Wall Street Journal, "the Moscow summit marks the beginning of the end of the Reagan era."[191] And so it did. Much had been accomplished at Moscow, but much more had to be deferred for a future summit agenda. Progress had been made incrementally on peripheral and largely functional issues that had come to a head in agreement and could be signed at Moscow. Differences on arms control, however, could not be composed and so remained to fuel the continuing dialogue, but with only minimal expectations that a START treaty could be signed at a possible fifth summit before the end of the Reagan Administration. One senior official cautioned about the need for time, patience and perspective in negotiating with the Soviets. "If you're going to start having summit meetings every six months or a year," he said somewhat apologetically regarding the limited achievements at Moscow, "you can't run it like the World Series. You can't expect to have a big result every time." Still, he added approvingly, "It's good for the relationship to be regularized."[192]

(2) Arms Control, an Unmovable Obstacle. Both Gorbachev and Reagan professed their intention of concluding a START treaty at Moscow, but to

no avail. "Some useful progress was made in the last four days on some net-tlesome issues, like mobile missiles," noted Michael R. Gordon of The New York Times in a summary analysis of the negotiations. But, he said, there was "no narrowing of differences over the 'Star Wars' missile defense program or the sea-launched cruise missiles."[193]

In sum, major differences persisted on a number of key issues including, the interpretation of the ABM Treaty (the Soviets insisting on a strict con-struction that would limit testing, the Americans urging a loose construction that would permit wider testing of SDI); agreements on future research, test-ing, development, and deployment of space-based ballistic missile defenses; limits on mobile ICBMs; limits on submarine-launched cruise missiles (SLCMs) and verification procedures.[194]

By the time of the Moscow Summit, Gordon noted, both sides had worked out "the main outlines of a strategic arms treaty, including the combined ceil-ing that would be set on warheads and cruise missiles, limits that would be set on warheads on ballistic missiles and some general ideas for how to go about verifying a strategic arms treaty." "But filling in the blanks," Gordon observed, required "a lot of negotiating on highly technical issues, as well as a yet-to-be achieved breakthrough over 'Star Wars' testing." No breakthroughs were anticipated before the Moscow meeting, and none were achieved: The negotiators returned home empty-handed.[195]

In March, when agreement was reached on convening a summit meeting in Moscow and after two days of intensive negotiating on START with Secretary Shultz, Soviet Foreign Minister Shevardnadze said of the work ahead on concluding a START treaty, "It is not an easy task. It is very com-plicated. There are many problems of a technical nature, but in principle it can be done. We are convinced it is possible."[196]

Differences in START proved to be too great and problems too difficult for the Moscow negotiators; agreement could not be reached; the issue was deferred. Howard Baker seemed to reflect the decline in confidence that permeated the summiteers when he told an ABC News interviewer on June 1, "The odds on finishing a treaty in this term are probably no better than 50-50."[197] General Powell reflected an even more cautious and less hope-ful appraisal of the prevailing pessimistic mood among some on the U.S. delegation when he said with respect to concluding a strategic arms pact against the opposition of "conservative lawmakers": "We have to take this slowly; it is too important to rush. In the next six months, the next six years, if you don't come home with a treaty that the experts, the Congress, don't see as strong, it'll never be ratified."[198]

Thus the unresolved issue of strategic arms control was deferred for sometime in the future, much to the disappointment of a Gorbachev "ex-tremely eager" to complete the treaty and at least to some American negotiators.[199] But that is the nature of negotiations and diplomacy. They lend themselves naturally to the process of incrementalism. Immovable objects sometimes defy the physics and dynamics of bargaining. Solutions often come slowly — sometimes not at all, and the management of issues takes time, work, study, infinite patience, wisdom and good luck. Successful bargaining on a strategic arms pact would have to wait a more propitious historic moment when, like the INF Treaty, the interests of both sides coalesce and immovable objects can give way to the rationality and argument of persistent negotiators.

2.   As a Negotiating Encounter

a.   Pre-Conference Jockeying for Position

(1) Focusing on the Agenda. Traditionally, negotiations do not really begin when the interlocutors sit down at the bargaining table. Rather they begin during the period well before the formal opening of negotiations when the competing sides maneuver politically in countless ways to create a negotiating environment favorable to one side and disadvantageous to the other. The prior announced Soviet withdrawal from Afghanistan, for example, had a decided effect on negotiating regional issues at Moscow adding to Soviet credibility in world public opinion. In brief, the pressure to influence begins early and is often applied with vigor. The Moscow Summit was no exception to this general rule as both sides energetically jockeyed for position on the eve of the meeting in Moscow.

The central focus of both Gorbachev's and Reagan's strategy during the pre-conference maneuvering was the agenda: Each sought to spotlight the single issue uppermost in their own negotiating strategy. For Gorbachev it was the necessity of progress in a strategic arms agreement; for Reagan it was advancing the democratic principles bound up in the human rights issue. Both were in agreement on the transcending value of summitry in stabilizing the relationship through a continuation of the diplomatic dialogue and in a larger sense by codifying the progress made as a result of four summit meetings.

(2) Gorbachev's Pitch for Agreement on Strategic Arms. Gorbachev made his most energetic pitch for a strategic arms agreement in an extraordinary interview with The Washington Post published on May 22. The General Secretary made it transparently clear that he would hold firm to his main positions in the negotiations for a strategic arms agreement. He insisted that such a long-range arms accord could not be concluded unless both sides agreed on a strict interpretation of the 1972 ABM Treaty that in effect would put sharp limits on tests for the President's highly prized SDI and antimissile program.

"If we just replace one kind of arms race with another, particularly in space, where the arms race would take a particularly dramatic turn," the Soviet leader forcefully argued "we would undermine the trust that has begun to be built; we would make worthless all the experience that we have accumulated at the Geneva negotiations." He also stressed the need to set limits on sea-launched cruise missiles that are armed with nuclear warheads. Unless limits were set, he warned, these missiles "would also be a new round-about maneuver that could become a new avenue for the arms race."

Perhaps Gorbachev's sharpest thrust was made when he commented on moving the arms race into space. If this were done, he warned, it would take decades "to reach some kind of agreement." And he then added this sharp stricture against those who would take such a course directing his attack clearly at the President:

> I think that he who pushes for an arms race in space is committing a crime against the people – his own people, and others. That must be said with all responsibility, and with clarity. Such an approach, such an idea, is a road to destabilization, to unpredictability on matters of security. This must be condemned, the initiator of such an approach must be pilloried.[200]

Whether by coincidence or design, the Gorbachev interview was published on the day before senior Reagan Administration officials were preparing for a White House meeting to review what arms control positions to take at the Moscow meeting.[201]

(3) Reagan's Pressuring on Human Rights. Reagan's jousts with Gorbachev on the human rights issue began in April when he made three speeches pointedly criticizing the Soviet Union for its failure to allow greater freedom of expression. Gorbachev sharply rebutted the President's charges, calling his tone "confrontational," and added with an air of finality: "We have so far been showing restraint, but if we reciprocate – and we can do so over a very wide range of issues – the atmosphere in Soviet-American relations can become such that it will make it no longer possible to solve any further issues."[202]

Opportunities abounded for the President to make known publicly his insistence on making human rights a principal item on the superpower agenda: a pre-summit interview over Worldnet USIA's global network; his departure statement from the White House lawn; an interview by Soviet journalists at the White House before leave for Helsinki and aired over Soviet television on May 28; and a pretaped broadcast aired on the 28th from Helsinki.

But it was the meeting in Finlandia Hall in Helsinki to celebrate the 13th anniversary of the signing of the Helsinki Final Act on human rights that provided the main stage for the President to make his case. His remarks were geared to a global audience, but his main target was Moscow. In a major address the President explored at length the matter of human rights as a problem in contemporary international relations. He expressed his satisfaction that human rights had become "an integral component" of the superpower agenda, and he praised the General Secretary for the progress achieved thus far in his reform program of glasnost and perestroika, citing such positive signs as release of prisoners from labor camps or exile, the publication of books heretofore proscribed, and the beginning withdrawal from Afghanistan. But he added this pointed criticism:

> All this is new and good. But at the same time, there is another list, defined not by us but by the standards of the Helsinki Final Act and the sovereign choice of all participants, including the Soviet Union, to subscribe to it. We need look no further through the Final Act to see where Soviet practice does not — or does not yet — measure up to Soviet commitment.

The President then proceeded to cite significant Soviet violations such as the failure to resolve cases of divided families, continued restrictions on emigration, and the failure to release people in jail "for expression of political or religious belief, or for organizing to monitor the Helsinki Act."[203]

In brief, the President took full advantage of his "bully pulpit" to make his case on human rights and thereby add pressure to the Soviet side. Both Gorbachev and Reagan thus engaged in a good deal of pre-summit maneuvering, attempting to pressure each other on points of vulnerability before opening negotiations in Moscow. Such practice can be viewed as not exceptional but rather as a normal part of the negotiating process.

b.   Planning on the U.S. Side

(1) Human Rights, Pomp, Ceremony and Symbolism. As a former actor and now a public figure, the President had come to look upon major public events as dramatic happenings that had to be skillfully crafted and carefully carried out with an eye to effect and dramatic impact. He had a dramatic presence — a sense of the dramatic moment — that stamps events with a certain appealing authenticity that attracts attention. The Moscow Summit was such a public event — such a dramatic moment — and was so organized, no doubt with the added thought that this was the President's final performance before departing from the international stage.

Presidential aides charged with planning the Moscow trip determined from the start that human rights, defined in the broader sense of political, economic, social, intellectual and religious freedom, would be the central theme around which speeches, press conferences and other events, public and private, requiring Presidential participation and appearances would be structured. One observer later fittingly referred to the Moscow meeting as "the human rights summit."[204]

Presumably after the March meeting between Shevardnadze and Shultz when attempts to clear away the last remaining obstacles to START had failed again, the expectation set in more earnestly on the U.S. side that Moscow would be a summit of symbolism, pomp and ceremony. As the London Economist opined, "Nobody expects the Moscow summit to produce either a new idea or a new treaty to be signed by the two leaders,"[205] and as Steven V. Roberts of The New York Times reported, the Moscow meeting "is expected to be heavy with symbolism and ceremony."[206]

Accordingly, it was reported that Presidential aides set out to construct a summit scenario and write a script that would resemble an American political campaign with strong emphasis on visual impressions and the emotional impact the President would generate among the Soviet people. Wanting to go from the President's strengths, they determined to emphasize his "incomparable" skill in carrying out the ceremonial functions of the Presidency, while playing down what was perceived as a major weakness, "his reputed failure to grasp and explain the details of public policy." As a recognized "great communicator," the planners intended to stress the oral as well as the visual, having in mind Gorbachev's successful public relations campaign during the Washington Summit. As Tom Griscom, the director of White House communications and chief planner of the trip, said, "Many times, the visual image of the President is as important as the words he speaks." The President communicates best, he said, when he goes out "where the people are, to meet people on their own terms. We're going to put the President in their environment, where they work and where they live."[207]

(2) Detailed Planning by Presidential Aides. Upon returning from Moscow the President compared his fourth meeting with Gorbachev to an epic film by the legendary Hollywood producer Cecil B. DeMille and said that he felt like he had been "dropped into a grand historical moment." In retrospect, the summit was an important historical moment, perhaps not "grand," but as the Soviets would say, "it was not by chance." For as the President's planners went about their pre-conference work they left little to chance. The White House planning group was headed by Griscom and General Powell. They worked for three months to create an advance script that one senior U.S. official said was intended to be "coherent and convincing." The degree of detailed planning for such a major diplomatic event was said to be "unprecedented" in the Reagan Administration. Competing agencies within the Administration, often at odds, cooperated fully in making the arrangements.[208]

The first step in the process was to create a "focus group" of suburban Philadelphia voters late in February as a testing ground for principal themes in the President's presentations. Assembled by Richard B. Wirthlin, a public opinion specialist, the "focus group" found that voters favored the President's efforts to improve superpower relations and liked Gorbachev, though they remained suspicious of Soviet intentions. "We didn't let the survey drive our effort," said Griscom, "but it was good to know that the people approved of the President's idea of building a brighter future in a safe world." "Much of our emphasis on people-to-people programs which the President emphasized came out of the survey group," he continued, noting approvingly that, "This idea has much favor with the American people."

In their initial planning, the Presidential aides focused on the period from mid-May through early June as the possible time of the meeting. Early in February, Griscom, Powell, and Howard Baker met with the President to discuss the content of the prospective summit. "The President wanted direct contact with the Soviet people," said Griscom. Wirthlin initiated a public opinion survey, and the Philadelphia "focus group" meeting was held just before the President's trip to NATO headquarters in Brussels. As he flew back to Washington on March 3, the summit advance team left for Moscow.

Before the advance team left, however, Griscom, James L. Hooley, director of the advance team, and Jack L. Courtemache, chief of staff for Nancy Reagan, had outlined 20 prospective events. The Soviets were said to be "cooperative," assuring the U.S. officials that, in the words of the press report, they wanted "the Reagans to feel comfortable with the schedule." The advance team returned through Helsinki, where the President would spend four days, and stopped off in London where he would conclude the nine-day trip.

On March 15, Griscom and Powell again met with Chief of Staff Baker and then conferred with the President. By the time of the Shevardnadze-Shultz meeting on March 23, when the exact dates were set, prospective events in Moscow were already being planned. On the following day, the advance team returned to the Soviet Union with a summit script that included the events that were to actually take place, except for one of the four Gorbachev-Reagan meetings, a dinner at the Gorbachev dacha, and the President's walk through Arbat. Griscom, it was reported, had no problems dealing with the Soviets. To his surprise they answered all questions on the spot, avoiding written replies; they agreed to two dinners, an arrival and departure ceremony and other meetings that were similar to the Washington Summit which served as the American model.

In the meantime, the White House speechwriting team went to work preparing 14 sets of remarks the President would make over a 10-day period beginning with his departure comment from the south lawn of the White House on May 25. The speechwriters placed a major emphasis on three speeches in this order: a May 27 address in Helsinki, emphasizing human rights; a May 31 speech at Moscow State University, praising the value and virtues of human liberty; and a June 3 speech at Guildhall where the President would sum up developments in Soviet-American relations. Griscom explained:

> We had three stops and three basic speeches. We asked State to give us a policy outline for each speech, each stop. The Moscow address contained a speech within a speech because the President wanted it to be a civics lesson for Soviet students. He wanted to talk about America and about Americans.

The speechwriting team was headed by Anthony Dolan who is described as a "conservative." Dolan often skirmished with the State Department and was said to have "drawn fire from moderates in the administration for provocative expressions of Reagan views." In preparing their speeches the writers immersed themselves in Russian history and culture in an effort to provide what was described as "authentic speeches." The speeches were sprinkled with Russian proverbs and quotations from famous Russian writers and poets. Some came from the speechwriters; other from the Librarian of Congress James H. Billington, an historian of Russian culture.

In preparing the final speeches Griscom and Powell were confronted with two drafts: the State Department drafts that, in the words of a senior official familiar with the process, were in language "suitable for publication in some obscure journal," and drafts by White House speechwriters that "reflected Reagan's views but didn't understand all the diplomatic consideration." The final product, said the official, "met the considerations of diplomacy and the President's strongly held convictions" on various issues, notably human rights. Differences over content in most of the speeches were ironed out amicably.

Not so the Helsinki speech that produced what one official called a "tug of war" between Thomas W. Simons, Jr., the State Department's senior authority on Soviet affairs, and "conservative" White House speechwriter Clark Judge. Simons contended that the White House draft was too confrontational on human rights and inappropriate as a presidential scene-setter for the summit. Judge contended that the President should not pull his punches on human rights issues, especially in the symbolic forum that Helsinki represented; for it was the Helsinki Final Act and subsequent negotiations in the Conference on Security and Cooperation in Europe (CSCE) that directed international attention to the human rights issue. Both protagonists were permitted to "fight it out," resolving differences finally through compromise and intervention by Powell and Griscom. The result was one that both could live with: It attempted to strike a balance in an unusually detailed recitation of Gorbachev's reform efforts with strong criticism of continuing Soviet human rights violations.

(3) Successful Execution. Emphasis on human rights had won the praise of American conservatives[209] and supporters of human rights causes but drew sharp criticism, as noted above, from the Soviets and particularly from Gorbachev. Soviet Deputy Foreign Minister Bessmertnykh plainly disliked the President's stress on human rights and laid the blame for his "error in judgment" on his advisers who prepared him for the Moscow trip. In a post-summit assessment over Moscow's Studio 9 television program, Bessmertnykh charged:

> I think Reagan was being prepared to think that he was being awaited here in the Soviet Union as almost some kind of messiah who would bring the Soviet people some kind of truth about human rights. Obviously, he was fed this [by "those who prepared him"], and his last speeches in Finland, made in Helsinki on the eve of his visit, showed that he was inclined to think this way. I think that this was one of the big mistakes made by the President on this issue.[210]

With respect to the planning of the summit recorded in an unusual press account, there seems little doubt that the President's aides were on target. In a summit that was expected to produce little substance, pomp, ceremony and symbolism were in order particularly when they could be orchestrated to put the President at best advantage and to fulfill his wishes of wanting direct exposure and close-in contact with the Soviet people.

Similarly, the President's speeches were skillfully designed to serve his purpose of emphasizing the human values of political liberty, religious toleration, economic, social and intellectual freedom. What made the speeches especially important is that they combined three vital elements necessary for official presentation: official policy, thoughts and genuine beliefs of the President, and the rhetoric of skilled writers fitting for the President's personality and style. Together they permit an effective form of official communication in that they are authoritative and appealing — universally, it might be said, not only to the ear but to the mind and heart. And in the person of a widely recognized skillful communicator and successful political campaigner this is an asset of considerable magnitude in negotiating at the summit.

c.   Organizing the Conference

(1) Logistics: Providing the Necessities and Comforts of Office and Home. One of the most difficult tasks for the White House planners was to arrange logistical support for the President and his supporting staff. To do this they

created a mini-White House on the Moskva, 5,000 miles from the Potomac.[211]

The temporary White House at Spaso House provided the President and his senior aides with all the facilities needed to run the U.S. Government and support the negotiators at the bargaining table. Thus arrangements were made, among other routine presidential activities, for bills to be signed and intelligence briefings on global affairs to be delivered at the customary hour of 9:00 a.m. Always close to the President in Moscow was a soft black leather briefcase known as "the football." In Moscow, it was carried by Air Force Major Steven Chealander. The briefcase contained the ultra secret codes and other material necessary to transmit orders-to-launch U.S. nuclear missiles and bombers, should the need arise.

Special provisions were made to protect communications against Soviet penetration. Signs were posted everywhere the summit party resided or worked — in hotel rooms, corridors and temporary offices, reminding staff, "This area is not safe for sensitive conversation or reading of classified material."[212] Not far from the embassy is a church that U.S. officials believed to be a center for intelligence gathering. Among U.S. residents it is known as, "Our Lady of Telemetry."

With such security concerns in mind two recreational vehicles, shielded to protect against electronic penetration, were parked in the embassy garage for use by Secretary Shultz and National Security Adviser Powell. One was installed for secure conversations, including those on telephones; the other to receive and send secure information. White House staffers used Soviet cars ("Not particularly" comfortable. "They're a low-rent model") and drivers[213]; the President and a few other officials had their own cars with U.S. drivers. So as not to compromise their colleagues and protect them against potential blackmail, White House staff members avoided what was described as "their normal pattern of in-house gossip."[214]

Much of the equipment and supporting gear were airlifted to Moscow on C-5A Air Force transports, the largest airplane in the West. Among the material provided was the President's armored limousine with back-up and Secret Service follow-on van. In addition, special airlifts were provided to transport everything from photocopiers to desks, from crockery to light bulbs. Fearful of not having "all the comforts of home," staff planners provided for such common household items as shower curtains (not available in Moscow), soap (the Soviet brand was judged inadequate), water to insure against stomach upset, toilet paper and facial tissues. All the food for the Spaso House dinner for the Gorbachevs, including lobster bisque, sesame sticks, supreme of chicken with truffle sauce, on to frozen chocolate mousse with vanilla sauce, and California wines, was flown in from the United States. Also made available for the Americans were such notable American delicacies as doughnuts, ham-and-cheese and turkey-and-cheese sandwiches served in the mini-White House mess set up for staffers staying at the Mezhdunarodnaya Hotel.

In sum, nothing was lacking to insure the efficiency and serve the comfort of the visiting Americans, from office supplies unavailable to them in Moscow to the simple items that would insure personal comfort. Being on their own territory, the Soviets had no such logistical needs to fulfill, and apparently responded favorably to satisfy American requests.

(2) Staffing. An estimated 600 officials constituted the U.S. delegation, including technical support staff tasked to handle transportation, communications and security. White House aides acknowledged that feelings were hurt and egos bruised among those who wanted to attend but were excluded owing to space limitations.[215]

Among the principal officials who accompanied the President included, from the White House, Howard H. Baker, Jr., Chief of Staff, Kenneth M. Duberstein, his deputy, Griscom and Fitzwater, the press secretary; from the National Security Council, General Powell, Col. Robert E. Linhard, special assistant to the President for arms control, along with other arms control advisers and one Soviet specialist; from the State Department, the Secretary, Michael H. Armacost, Undersecretary for Political Affairs, other regional assistant secretaries, Max M. Kampelman, the chief arms negotiator, and Paul H. Nitze, another leading specialist on arms control; and from the Defense Department, Secretary Carlucci and Richard L. Armitage, Assistant Secretary for International Security Affairs.[216]

The organization of the conference took on the structure of the four-point agenda, for example, with Soviet Marshal Akhromeyev and Nitze heading the working groups on arms control; Ridgway and Bessmertnykh heading the groups dealing with human rights; and Assistant Secretary of State Chester A. Crocker and Deputy Foreign Minister Anatoly L. Adamishin heading the group dealing with regional conflicts, notably Southern Africa.[217] Since this conference dealt with a wide range of issues in East-West relations, the presence of more supporting specialists and advisers was required than at the previous three summits,[218] along with talented specialists in foreign and national security policy drawn from appointed officials of the Reagan Administration and from the Government bureaucracy. One source referred to Reagan's foreign policy team that would be at his side as being "high-powered" and a "highly professional team oriented less toward ideology than toward achieving pragmatic results that will help keep U.S.-Soviet relations on a steady, improving course."[219]

Bessmertnykh, who was a close-in observer and participant on the Soviet side, gave an unusual and perceptive appraisal of some of these officials in his appearance on Studio 9 of June 11, 1988. To capture and preserve the authentic flavor of his appraisal the entire segment is quoted:

[Zorin] In this connection, I have a question for you as a person who saw it all from the inside. You have touched on it. What was Reagan's team like, and how was the work organized during the meeting?

[Bessmertnykh] Well, Reagan's team was well known to us. Valentin Mikhaylovich already spoke about one member of the team, Carlucci — by the way, an interesting metamorphosis. When Carlucci was in the White House as the President's national security adviser, Shultz brought him along regularly to talks, be they in Washington, Moscow, or Geneva. On the whole, he was a man of balanced views, at least in terms of what he said about Soviet-U.S. relations. When he went over to the Pentagon and became the secretary of defense, he became a totally different Carlucci. In one of the discussions, one of our representatives said to him: See how the positions spoils the man. But on the whole, this a man who is very experienced. He is also the former chief of the CIA [title as heard].

[Falin, interrupting] It is a means of transportation. If we were to place a doctor in a tank, he too would start to think differently.

[Bessmertnykh] Shultz is undoubtedly a figure who plays a serious role in world politics. They are all conservatives; he is, too. However, he is perhaps the most realistic in his appraisals of U.S. capabilities, which is very important for American politicians. As a rule, they do not have the ability to correctly assess their own capabilities and tend to exaggerate them. The same applies to his appraisal of the Soviet Union. Americans, as a rule, attempt to understate Soviet capabilities. Shultz, I feel, was able, to a large extent, to capture the balance of our interests, which no doubt was helpful. Powell, the current national security adviser, a three star Army general, is apparently more capable as a diplomat then a general. He has a soft, thoughtful appearance, and this seems to have appealed to the current President. He seems to be above party and politics. By the way, no one seems to know whether he belongs to the Democratic or the Republican Party. It seems that for this position, party affiliation is of no importance. More than that, it is important that no one knows about it. Howard Baker, the current White House chief of staff, is a man of much experience. He is a former leading senator who, not long ago, entertained presidential ambitions but now seems to have renounced them. Nevertheless, it seems that he will continue to play a serious role. By all appearances, he exerts consequential influence on the President. As far as a professional diplomat like Ridgeway, U.S. Assistant secretary of state for Europe and the Soviet Union [title as heard], is concerned, she is a diplomat with broad experience, and she was responsible for most of the work of drawing up joint documents. So, ideologically, the team was much as expected. It was conservative, highly professional, and pragmatic as a whole. A team which certainly gave support to the President at the talks, particularly in the Kremlin—I cannot say how they acted during discussions in the White House. Therefore, it could be said that Reagan leaned on a very strong team. The Soviet delegation had a worthy opponent, and, therefore, the discussions were profound and interesting.

[Falin] In the interest of reaching an agreement, perhaps a worthy partner is a better choice of words.[220]

Similarly, the Soviet delegation was made up of some of the Soviet Union's leading authorities in foreign and national security affairs. In addition to Shevardnadze, Bessmertnykh and others mentioned above, there were such notables as Gromyko, Alexander N. Yakovlev, Secretary of the CPSU Central Committee and close adviser to Gorbachev; Minister of Defense Dimitri T. Yazov; Dobrynin and Yuri V. Dubinin, the Soviet Ambassador to the United States. In light of the restructuring and professional up-grading within the Ministry of Foreign Affairs and the growing prominence of the institutes in Soviet foreign policy, it can be assumed that highly competent higher and mid-to-lower echelon Soviet staff, along with back-up from the institutes and their highly qualified staff, were close at hand to support the principal Soviet officials.[221]

(3) Informal Probing; Post-Conference Briefings. A principal feature of diplomatic gatherings such as the Moscow Summit is the degree of political exchange that goes on informally beyond the formal negotiating table. Social events provide an important setting for such informal probing. Sources on the Moscow Summit cite one such incident that took place at the state dinner in the Kremlin on May 30. Secretary Carlucci had firmly insisted throughout the negotiations with Defense Minister Yazov that SLCMs should not figure in calculations of the overall balance of destructive power. Yazov argued just as insistently on the Soviet side: SLCMs can strike deep inside the Soviet Union, he argued, and accordingly must be limited by START. At the Soviet-hosted state dinner in the Kremlin a civilian aide to Gorbachev "buttonholed" Marshal Akhromeyev, the principal authority on arms control in the Soviet leadership. It will be recalled that Gorbachev was anxious to conclude a START treaty in 1988 before the political uncertainties of the American presidential election set in. Why not put the SLCM issue aside for the moment, the aide said, thus allowing START to go forward. Talbott, who recorded the incident, wrote, "Nyet! boomed the marshal."[222] The probe failed; the Soviet position remained fixed.

Finally, both sides, following what was by now customary procedures, undertook briefings of their political allies. The President reported to Prime Minister Thatcher, while Secretary Shultz briefed NATO allies.[223] On the Soviet side, special representatives of the General Secretary visited a number of foreign countries and in the course of conversations with party, state leaders and other statesmen briefed them on the meeting. Among those briefed were East European leaders along with Chinese Deputy Foreign Minister Tian Zhenpei.[224]

d.   Role of the Media

(1) "Open" Media Coverage. When Bessmertnykh remarked on the Studio 9 telecast that "this summit was one of the most open meetings ever. . . our Soviet people and the foreign public saw almost everything," he was not exaggerating.[225] In keeping with glasnost, the Soviets opened up floodgates of information to the world media and provided unprecedented access for coverage by the 5,000 accredited correspondents. As Time magazine noted, "the Soviets put on an impressive show of *glasnost* for the world press."[226] Said ABC News Executive Producer William Lord who had been in Moscow on four different occasions, "Moscow is right now an open city. . . . It is just as open as Washington, D.C., is."[227]

The Soviets had also gone "to extraordinary lengths to make life easy for pampered Western journalist," reported David Remnick of The Washington Post from Moscow. They replicated as best they could the press center at the Washington Summit located in Moscow's Mezhdunarodnaya Hotel. Remnick writes that the resident correspondents "have been stunned by the clear phone connections courtesy of AT&T and the constant flow of briefing papers and pool reports provided by the White House press office."[228] And as for the Soviets, Remnick noted, they "are trying desperately and earnestly to keep up with the American competition, sending out long, if carefully edited, transmissions on the Soviet airwaves."

Not all reporters were so impressed. "This is like Ted Mack's amateur hour," said P.J. O'Rourke of Rolling Stone. "They run this press center like the event in question is the New York state hamster and gerbil show." But Martin Walker, Moscow reporter for the British Manchester Guardian for four years, countered, "What our visiting colleagues don't realize is that this may be the most organized operation in the history of the U.S.S.R."[229]

Access was clearly the operating word for the Soviet side. Gennadi Grasimov, the spokesman for the Ministry of Foreign Affairs, and Marlin Fitzwater, his counterpart in the White House, described with some wit as "the Alphonse and Gaston of bilateral relations," kept the media informed on the proceedings in regularly scheduled press briefings. Soviet public figures were also available to the media. They wandered through the press center offering comments on all manner of subjects. Gorbachev held a two-hour press conference, the first he had ever conducted in Moscow. Soviet officials staged a press conference for Andrei Sakharov, the celebrated scientist-dissident recently freed from internal exile by Gorbachev, and even arranged an interview for the BBC, CBS and ABC with Boris Yeltsin, Gorbachev's potential competitor who was removed as Moscow's Communist Party boss in November 1987.[230] Dan Rather of CBS was able to have an informal and unscheduled on-the-spot three-minute interview with Gorbachev in the Kremlin's Cathedral Square, employing many of the aggressive tactics learned in his early days of television journalism to seize this unique opportunity. A short time later, Steve Hurst, Moscow bureau chief for the Cable News Network (CNN), "snared" a Gorbachev interview in much the same way, as the Soviet leader was leaving one meeting for another.[231]

"All in all," concluded Time in a summary statement on media coverage in Moscow, "it was an amazing lesson on the new scope of *glasnost* and also on its limits."[232]

U.S. coverage of the summit was extensive, both by print and television journalists. Among the U.S. television luminaries reporting from Moscow were Peter Jennings of ABC, Tom Brokaw of NBC, and Dan Rather of CBS. CNN cable news was on the scene giving its extensive coverage. Television critic Tom Shales noted, "Since the weekend, when coverage began in earnest, all the networks have carried remarkable sights and sound," using the best available communications technology. "Openness to outside media," he continued, "is unprecedented and, all things considered, breathtaking." "The Soviets clearly have learned a great deal about press relations and, if you will, press manipulation," said Rather. "And they have clearly changed their attitude about what they want their image to be on television." Timothy Russert, an NBC News executive vice president, commented on Soviet media behavior:[233]

> All the networks have used the summit as an opportunity to gain access to people and places we've never had before. . . . We've all capitalized on it enormously. . . . Soviet rulers are growing in their sophistication about the media. That modifies their behavior. You can see a dramatic difference in the way they conduct themselves. They know the whole world is watching, and they are on their best behavior.

On the Soviet side, the coverage seemed to be massive. While avoiding controversial subjects almost entirely, the evening news program Vremya gave what was described as "voluminous" coverage to the summit. Vremya is said to have more viewers than any other news program in the world. Repetition is apparently a normal practice in coverage of such major events as summits. Full and repeated coverage was given, for example, to the complete renditions of both national anthems played at the airport on the President's arrival and to the complete dinner speeches by Gorbachev and Reagan at the state dinner—just the sort of thing, writes Remnick, "that is known politely at American networks as 'death'." A graphic appraisal of comparative coverage seemed to be close to the mark when Jonathan Sanders, a Columbia University professor and special correspondent for CBS news, observed, "American coverage is like neat little scatter rugs." "The Soviets," he noted, "are going for the wall-to-wall carpeting approach."[234]

Moreover, the Soviets called into play some of their leading scholars, commentators, foreign affairs specialists and officials to discuss the proceedings during and after the summit over Soviet television, radio and in the press for the better understanding, and edification, of the Soviet citizenry. The U.S. Foreign Broadcast Information Service (FBIS) published three separate special annexes on the summit, in addition to other extensive material, that contain full texts and excerpts from Soviet programs and press coverage. The sheer volume and quality of the coverage was impressive.

In brief, Soviet media saturation of the Moscow Summit seemed to be complete.

(2) Restricting and Distorting the Reagan Message. Notwithstanding the outpouring of media coverage on the summit, it was—at the Soviet end—selective and manipulated, particularly with respect to comments by the President on such sensitive subjects as human and religious rights. In a post-summit audit of Soviet media coverage, FBIS gave this summary analysis:

> The majority of the President's speeches, including his remarks in those speeches on sensitive issues, were reported fully in Soviet media. However, his remarks on such occasions were reported only selectively and in two instances virtually not at all. Extensive commentary on the President's speeches designed either to counter his remarks or explain them in the context of official policy confirms that Soviet media, while increasingly serving as sources of information, have not abandoned their traditional role of serving as channels for the dissemination of official views.[235]

Though the President and the General Secretary were "featured performers" over Vremya's evening news, many of the carefully crafted words of the President had never actually reached the Soviet public. For example, Vremya gave extended coverage on May 31 containing extensive reports and pictures of the President's day. But the broadcast dropped his references at the writers' club to censorship in the Soviet Union and to exiled Soviet dancers and musicians in America who the President had said he hoped would someday return to Moscow and perform. Vremya also showed a picture of the President speaking on democracy to students at the Moscow State University, but provided only a carefully edited summary—"snippets," one report said—of his comments in a voice-over report by the announcer. "Evidently," the press report concluded with accuracy and truth, "the new policy of *glasnost* (openness) does not extend to a crusading U.S. president in Moscow."[236]

Not only did the Soviets carefully screen the President's words in media coverage of his speeches, but they also countered his criticism of Soviet human rights violations by staging their own countering events such as the press conference of dissenting American Indians.[237] They also denounced in their media some of the guests among the dissidents at the Spaso House meeting with the President, one of whom, Nikolai Roshko, was identified as a convicted wartime collaborator with the Germans.[238]

(3) Reflections on Media Coverage: Soviet Progress and Reaction to Reagan. Soviet media coverage of the Moscow Summit suggests that the Soviets have been on an ascending curve of improvement since their first major media undertaking of the Gorbachev era at the Geneva Summit of 1985.[239] They seem to have come a long way towards mastering the mechanics of media coverage, such as, the staging of press conferences and holding press briefings, having available knowledgeable authorities for press interviews, and establishing a functional press center.

The Moscow Summit was, moreover, a convincing example of glasnost in action on the international stage not only in its positive aspects for Western media coverage but also for a deeper understanding of the impact of a "good press" on advancing the goals of foreign policy. In his review of television coverage at Moscow, TV-critic Tom Shales makes this comment that underscores the positive side of glasnost as the Soviets see it and its uses in the conduct of foreign policy:

> Shots of politicians cuddling babies are not usually hot stuff. But when the politicians are Mikhail Gorbachev and Ronald Reagan and they are cuddling the toddler in the middle of Red Square, the picture takes on a genial, symbolic momentousness. It's not just two men and a baby anymore.
>
> Gorbachev held the child and Reagan shook the boy's hand yesterday in one of the many benign, salubrious images to be beamed over by satellite from the U.S.S.R., where the networks are busily and rather gloriously covering the Moscow summit. The pictures say a new era in U.S.-Soviet relations is not mere illusion, and the access the American networks have had in the Soviet capital has been wildly encouraging, at least to them.[240]

Despite Soviet manipulation of the media, the President seems to have succeeded in making the positive impression on the Soviet people that his planners had hoped for. A review of press accounts, admittedly unscientific, suggests a divided opinion on the President's performance in Moscow. Some of the official commentators such as Vitali Kobysh, a former official of the Central Committee who now writes for Izvestia, said in what was described as "a harsh commentary" that, "The U.S. President no longer risks publicly calling us 'the evil empire.'. . . [He even] directs compliments in our direction — condescending compliments. I only fear that deep down, he hasn't changed his opinion about us."[241]

On the other hand, the general public reacted far more favorably to the President. "Among ordinary Muscovites who have not seen much" of the President, reported Bill Keller of The New York Times, the response was "warm and vague." Muscovites interviewed on June 1 revealed that they had "got a sense of Mr. Reagan's warmth and good will" and that his willingness to come to Moscow raised their hopes, but, according to Keller, "he remains largely a stranger." "We've moved beyond the stereotype," said Larissa Trublina. But like most of the 30 pedestrians interviewed, she could not clearly identify any particular thing except that he seemed "good willed" and had been sufficiently thoughtful to quote Russian proverbs.[242]

"What I have read a lot about Reagan is that he is fervent anticommunist," said Mikhail Vasyanin, a 20-year old student who heard the President speak at Moscow State University. "But if an anticommunist could speak so eloquently about principles that are important to us, too, that's impressive."[243]

Particularly appealing to Muscovites was the President's reference to Soviet women and his expressed concern that they deserve a great deal of credit. "I liked that," a female Moscow artist said the following day. "I wasn't expecting it."[244]

The general public's view of the President was in many respects one-dimensional. Understandably so, because the average Soviet citizen saw little of the real Reagan before or during his Moscow visit except for ceremonial occasions broadcast over television and sanitized excerpts from his speeches read in the press. Television coverage of the walkabout in Red Square showed the President and the General Secretary caressing a child in the universally appealing style of the politician. But his speeches to the students at Moscow University and members of the writer's club, received enthusiastically by the audience, were muted by Soviet failure to report them fully.

e.   Role of the First Ladies

(1) Politics, Tourism and Continuing "Feud". As at the Geneva and Washington Summits, the First Ladies, Raisa Gorbachev and Nancy Reagan,

played highly visible roles at the Moscow meeting, in contrast to the custom in the pre-Gorbachev era when the wives of the Soviet and American leaders stayed in the background if they were indeed present at all. The role of the present First Ladies was not specifically political in the sense of participating in any negotiations. Rather it was peripheral, but important, nonetheless, since it was one of providing visible support for their husbands and the policies they were pursing. In the case of Mrs. Reagan this was an especially important occasion because she was able by her words, actions, and very presence—carried over Soviet television and in the media—to accent the same themes that White House planners had laid out for the President. It will be recalled that Mrs. Reagan actually played a prominent role in the planning stage. To this extent her role was politically important.

Mrs. Reagan's itinerary took in visits to all the major tourist attractions in Moscow and Leningrad, such as, the Assumption Cathedral; the writers' colony of Peredelkino where Boris Pasternak is buried; the Hermitage Museum in Leningrad where she also laid a wreath at a memorial commemorating the defenders of the city and the 650,000 who perished during the 900-day Nazi siege in World War II; and the Tretyakov Gallery in Moscow. Visits to Soviet schools and cultural centers were also on the First Lady's schedule.[245]

What captured public attention, at least in the West, was not so much the role played by the First Ladies as the reports of the strained personal relationship that existed between them, commonly referring to it as a "feud" that began during their first meeting in Geneva in 1985, and heated up at the Washington Summit. As Felicity Barringer of The New York Times noted from Moscow, "Last December the frigid joint appearances of Mrs. Reagan and Mrs. Gorbachev lent credence to rumors of mutual dislike and disdain, rumors that eventually blossomed into cattiness. . . ."[246]

During the Moscow meeting a great deal of press attention was, therefore, focused on the personal relationship between the two First Ladies as journalists seemed to search desperately for evidence of a continuing "feud." But, at least at the beginning, Mrs. Gorbachev and Mrs. Reagan sought to silence such reports. When they met for the first time in Moscow beneath the gilded chandeliers in St. George's Hall, they smiled, in the words of Barringer, "with brittle cordiality," but "their stolid expressions melted into laughter" when they listened to their husbands' dueling proverbs. "By the time they emerged from the towering Assumption Cathedral," Barringer notes, "Nancy Reagan and Raisa Gorbachev were holding hands."[247]

Accounts of their cordial relationship continued until Mrs. Reagan's tour of the Tretyakov Gallery on Wednesday. Friction reportedly surfaced when in a seemingly inconsequential mixup of schedules Mrs. Reagan was late for the tour, and Mrs. Gorbachev, visibly annoyed, briefly carried on without her, delivering her remarks to the attending press corps. The gallery featured many icons, or works of religious art, and when Mrs. Gorbachev spoke of art only from an historical perspective ignoring the theological significance Mrs. Reagan, who finally arrived, interjected, as Mrs. Gorbachev "frowned at her watch", "I do not know how you can neglect the religious implications. I mean, they are there for everyone to see. I am impressed by their beauty."[248] When during an ensuing informal press conference Mrs. Reagan was asked about her impressions of communism, she respectfully responded, "We have two different ways of living. We have two different philosophies. That's not going to change." And she added, "I'd call it a Mexican standoff."[249] When reporters asked Elaine Crispen, Mrs. Reagan's press secretary, about the signs of tension and friction between the First Ladies, she replied diplomatically:

> Is it tension or friction? Or just two people who might not ordinarily seek each other out but have been put together because of what their husbands are trying to accomplish. There's no feud, but the two are from different worlds. . . . Each is doing her best to be gracious hostesses and guests in their respective countries.[250]

(2) First Ladies and Summitry: An Innovative Precedent? Perhaps Crispen's tactful explanation may come nearest the mark when probing the reason for the differences between the First Ladies. But this is only a superficial judgment at best, a pseudo-event generated by a conflict-seeking press. The real importance of their role is underscored in the last sentence — "Each is doing her best to be gracious hostesses and guests in their respective countries." For that is precisely what both ladies were trying to do. Theirs was essentially a political role, despite the veneer of hostility seen as enveloping the relationship, and was, therefore, an important part of the larger drama taking place in meetings and negotiations between the General Secretary and the President and their aides.

This seems to be the real meaning of the presence and the role of the First Ladies at the Moscow Summit. In this sense an innovative precedent, initiated in Geneva, may have been firmly established for the future; their presence could become a durable part of future summits.

f.   Formalities and Their Importance: Reinforcing
      the Traditions of Diplomacy

Moscow was a summit of ceremony and symbolism. From the moment the presidential party stepped off Air Force One at Vnukovo Airport on May 29 until its departure on June 2, official life was an unending procession of ceremony:

- the formal review of the Honor Guard by President Reagan and President Gromyko, walking as if in a close-order drill, with banners and flags flying and the military band playing the national anthems;
- the formal greeting by the General Secretary in St. George's Hall amid the pomp and splendor of the surroundings in the ancient Kremlin's Grand Palace;
- the state dinners with their lush banquet atmosphere, formal speeches by the General Secretary and the President and no doubt, except for Dave Brubeck, the American jazz pianist, stiffly formal entertainment;
- the ceremony of formally exchanging the documents of ratification of the INF Treaty by Gorbachev and Reagan and the signing of nine separate agreements by Secretary Shultz and Foreign Minister Shevardnadze; and on to the,
- final departure ceremony in St. George's Hall, again with formal speeches, the martial music and rigidly formal Honor Guard marching in review for both Presidents.

All of this splendor and ceremony was recorded on television and beamed throughout the Soviet Union, the United States, Europe, and the rest of the world. Detailed reports on the summit proceedings appeared in the world press. Coverage by the internationally prestigious The New York Times and The Washington Post was extensive, as was the case in Soviet media.

There was a purpose beneath this grand display. Tom Shales put his finger on it when he wrote of the Gorbachev-Reagan presence with a small child in Red Square, "the picture takes on a genial, symbolic momentousness. It's not just two men and a baby anymore. . . ." For this and the other pictures convey a very important political meaning: they "say a new era in U.S.-Soviet relations is not mere illusion. . . ."[251]

This public display symbolically in the very heart of the Soviet Union had, therefore, a larger meaning: It was meant to demonstrate before the whole world the seriousness of this diplomatic undertaking at Moscow and the deeper political purposes behind the policies that brought both leaders to the summit. When modern diplomatic practice was in its infancy during the early Modern Age, Kings and Princes, Popes and Pashas embellished such formal occasions as treaty signings and other state undertakings as a public display of intent: to underscore the seriousness of the undertaking; to give further legitimacy to the occasion by the solemnity surrounding the formalities of the event; and to generate a type of public pressure through this display to insure compliance and avoid public censure and scorn should the instrument be willfully violated.

The pomp and ceremony at Moscow served the same political purposes; it was solemnity in the service of political legitimacy.

Thus formalities, protocols and the ceremonial side of summitry have a unique value unto themselves. They impose on the proceedings values that have taken shape in the evolution of the modern diplomatic tradition. In summitry, therefore, form is substance. Form in this diplomatic setting requires civilized behavior in seeking the resolution of differences; it requires respect for law and custom, order and tradition in international society; it also requires a certain shared vision of mankind's future, if not in ultimate national goals, then at least in a mutually shared toleration of means to a particular end.

The Moscow Summit failed to resolve the most difficult arms control problem; namely, reduction of strategic weapons by 50 percent – though the issue remained alive and negotiable at some future time. But it succeeded, nonetheless, on lesser issues in contention. Compliance was, therefore, assured in many areas of mutual interest where conflict and dissonance had once reigned. But equally important, the Moscow Summit also succeeded in reinforcing the institution of summitry as a viable instrument of international relations. Accordingly, it contributed to preserving those forms of diplomacy that can insure a peaceful international society, at least between the superpowers who have the means of near-total global destruction. In contrast to the diplomacy of barbarism, as pursued by Hitler in the 1930s and early 1940s and by Stalin in the later Cold War years, a diplomacy that replaced respected formalities of traditional diplomacy with humiliation, denigration, and outright gangsterism, the diplomacy of the Moscow Summit represents a creative force in international society, a strengthening of negotiations and diplomacy as instruments of peace and a step forward towards a more peaceful and orderly world.

3. Gorbachev's and Reagan's Negotiating Performance

a. Conceptualizing a Negotiating Strategy

Diagnosis of differences, formulation of a principle that could constitute a basis for agreement, and conceptualization of a negotiating strategy are the initial requirements when adversaries enter negotiations.[252] Both Gorbachev and Reagan had undertaken these tasks in earnest since their meeting in Reykjavik during October 1986.

Gorbachev entered the Moscow negotiations, therefore, with a carefully conceived and oft proclaimed conceptualization of Soviet interests and goals. Briefly, they were to establish Soviet-American relations on a peaceful and stable basis through continuing dialogue and to achieve this goal through radical reductions in armaments. Gorbachev's ultimate negotiating aim called for a world free of nuclear weapons. The rationale dictating this negotiating strategy was the need to reduce external pressures so that much needed Soviet internal reform could go forward. Confrontation was to be replaced by dialogue and accommodation, expansionism by global retrenchment. Specifically, Gorbachev's central negotiating strategy was based on a principle that called for the reduction of strategic arms by 50 percent. The first step was already taken with the signing of the INF Treaty and the exchange of ratification instruments.

Reagan shared Gorbachev's adherence to the 50 percent reduction principle and the goal of a continuing dialogue. As he said at the White House departure ceremony, "My goal is to bequeath to my successor next January the firm basis for a stable, sustainable relationship with the Soviet Union."[253] But the President's conceptualization of the negotiation differed from Gorbachev's in one fundamental aspect; namely, his belief in the transcending importance of democratic human rights as a vital principle in international relations. Reagan's political beliefs, drawn from the traditions of Wilsonianism and proclaimed at Moscow with the fervor of a political evangelist, rest on the assumption that democracy is the key to success in generating national growth, achieving national political, social, and intellectual excellence, and attaining world peace. Democracy means economic freedom that generates the drive towards acquiring the benefits of the Scientific-Technological Revolution. But most of all democracy is the best assurance for world peace. Accordingly, Reagan linked internal reform in the Soviet Union, with its promise of greater freedom for the Soviet people, to improved possibilities for world peace. As he told the Soviet intellectuals at the Writer's House, "We believe that the greater the freedoms in our countries, the more secure both our own freedoms and peace."[254]

Thus, the vital center of Reagan's conceptualization of a negotiating strategy at Moscow was democratic human rights. The basic strategies of both interlocutors were, therefore, in conflict; only on peripheral issues was there agreement.

b.   Carrying Out Negotiating Strategies

(1) First Phase: Pre-Conference Maneuvering. As well-seasoned, skillful negotiators with a deep appreciation of negotiations as a process and craft, both the General Secretary and the President began carrying out their respective negotiating strategies well before their first formal meeting in Moscow. Clearly, they understood the necessity of making their negotiating points well in advance and seizing whatever initiatives were available for shaping the agenda and influencing the climate of negotiations in keeping with their strategies and expected outcomes. Both understood that negotiation is more than just bargaining across a table, but rather a process that

begins well before that operational phase. Accordingly, they lost no time in initiating the first phase of the process.

Gorbachev's extensive, informative, and penetrating interview in The Washington Post, examined above, is a remarkable example of the first phase of the General Secretary's negotiating strategy. The interview, constituting four solid pages of text of the interview and responses to questions submitted by the interviewers laid out in precise detail Gorbachev's agenda in order of priority and expected outcome, giving major prominence to the vital necessity of reaching agreement on reducing strategic arms. Here was an attempt through pre-conference maneuvering to seize the initiative, to alert the world as to what the Soviet Union expected from this meeting, and to impress upon world public opinion Soviet preferences. For The Washington Post is a prestigious international newspaper with high visibility in the capitals of the world.

Reagan exceeded Gorbachev in the extent of his pre-conference maneuvering. From his verbal jousts with Gorbachev in April, the White House departure speech among others, interviews with Soviet journalists and over Worldnet, and to his major address at the 13th anniversary ceremony of the Helsinki Final Act, the President hammered home his theme of democratic human rights as an essential ingredient in East-West relations, praising the Soviets for some progress but scolding them (politely) for their failures. There was no subtlety in his statement over Worldnet when he said of the connection between human rights and international relations, "It's not too much to say that the 1975 Final Act redefined East-West exchanges, enshrining human rights as an issue of *permanent* importance.[255]

Nothing was left to chance by either Gorbachev or Reagan. In pursuing the first phase of their negotiating strategies, both negotiators made sure their respective central themes were firmly imprinted on the public mind, and on that of the opposite side, well before the opening of the first formal bargaining session in Moscow.

(2) Attending to Externalities. During the five days of the summit meeting, both Gorbachev and Reagan continued to focus on the externalities of the negotiation. The intensity of their activities is recorded above.

In most of their public encounters, both leaders, judged by qualified observers to be natural political campaigners, shared the same platform and structured their comments to suit the occasion: the exchange of formal speeches upon Reagan's arrival and departure from Moscow, the toasts at the state dinners, and the walk through Red Square that produced a running dialogue — in which Gorbachev informally reiterated at one point Soviet negotiating priorities: "I can tell you that the problems of reducing strategic offensive weapons, interlinked with ABM, sea-based cruise missiles, and the problems of chemical weapons and conventional arms in Europe, are *central to our talks.*"[256]

On all occasions the General Secretary and the President exploited their opportunities to the fullest extent, and to magnify the impact, their performances were recorded on television and in the press. Gorbachev scored heavily in making his points on the necessity of arms control, while Reagan made the most of his "bully pulpit" to preach the virtues of human rights and to give his "civic lesson" to the Soviets on democracy. (One New York Times report from Moscow was headlined, "A Mighty Russian Pulpit for Reagan.")[257]

For Gorbachev, the final press conference provided a unique opportunity for giving his own assessment of the summit, something beyond the homogenized rhetoric of the final conference communique. In that free-wheeling, energetic encounter with the world press, the General Secretary forcefully registered his disappointment that an opportunity had been lost by the U.S. failure to be more forthright on such matters as strategic arms control. Compared with the vigor of this complaint, the pronouncements of his satisfaction with the meeting seemed to be proper but subdued. Another post-summit press conference, attended by some followers of the anti-nuclear movement, provided Gorbachev still another opportunity to reiterate his assessment. By this time the formal negotiations had ended and thus the time for exerting external pressures had passed. But the issues remained alive, nonetheless, for other expected encounters in the near future and thus served the useful purpose of keeping the Soviet agenda before the world public.

Like Gorbachev, Reagan also went to great lengths in his attempts to shape the externalities and accordingly influence the negotiations. His highly visible walk through the Arbat mall was a bold personal demonstration with clear political intent. But it was his speeches and meetings with the priests and believers at the Danilov Monastery, dissidents at Spaso House, Soviet intellectuals at the Writer's House, and students at Moscow State University that gave him the powerful and influential platforms he sought from which to plead his case for democracy and human rights. Subsequent speeches at Guildhall and Andrews Air Force Base echoed these familiar but lingering themes made in Moscow.

Thus Gorbachev and Reagan looked beyond the bargaining table in carrying out their negotiating strategies; for as popular communicators and skilled negotiators, widely recognized as such by qualified observers, they understood the importance of shaping the externalities of a negotiation so as to influence, if not to ensure, a favorable outcome at the actual bargaining table.

(3) At the Negotiating Table. (a) Agreement and Limited Sources. Sources on the actual negotiating sessions at Moscow are extremely limited, unlike the Geneva Summit where official sources were enriched by subsequent memoirs of participants and by very detailed press briefings of what took

place. The memoirs of the Moscow participants have yet to be written. And only bits and pieces of information are available as the result of persistent probing by enterprising reporters who through encounters in Moscow with the principals and their aides, along with formal press briefings, were able to provide some shafts of light in the contemporary press. No detailed, not-for-attribution briefings were held in the Geneva manner, hence the paucity of data.

In reality much of the political and diplomatic struggle actually took place beyond the negotiating table. This was the President's negotiating strategy. His mission, as he and his aides saw it, was more to influence the Soviet people than to sign diplomatic agreements, one of which relating to strategic arms control was not really expected.[258] Besides many of the agreements — "peanuts", as one aide described them — were already completed or in the final stages before the Moscow meeting. There was no drama to be exploited here.

Furthermore, many of the agreements fit neatly into Gorbachev's "new thinking" in foreign policy and thus were not matters of contention, but only refinement. Accordingly, harmony prevailed on many of the issues under discussion, and the actual negotiations themselves seemed to be mere formalities. This was true in such matters as student exchanges and cooperation in science and technology. More difficult was the negotiation on the Angolan issue, but even in this case, owing to selected Soviet retrenchment in the Third World as "new thinking" prescribes, agreement was reached in principle on the withdrawal of Cuban troops, an achievement of real substance.

Little was to be said or published, therefore, when negotiations led to quick and easy agreement. For conflict is the essence of news; it is that which makes an event newsworthy. No conflicts developed on the lesser issues; harmony reigned and thus no reason existed to report beyond favorable results. Real contention was reserved for human rights, strategic arms control, and the formulation of "peaceful coexistence," a long-standing key concept of Soviet foreign policy.

(b) Areas of Disagreement: Human Rights, "Peaceful Coexistence," and Strategic Arms Control. Gorbachev provided some glimpses into the negotiations when he complained about the failures of the summit at his June 1 press conference and in a subsequent address before peace activists in Moscow. As noted above, he was clearly annoyed at the President's preaching on human rights. Press accounts spoke of "barbed" exchanges on the issue; Howard Baker said that to Gorbachev the issue "strikes sparks." Publicly, Gorbachev was restrained in responding to the President, but in closed-door sessions with Reagan, according to one account, "he had been much more combative."[259]

"We had, for our part, decided to overcome our shyness and tact we had always shown when it came to human rights," the General Secretary said in a speech to international peace activists the day the President left Moscow. "We decided so because we had seen that it was harmful, that it did not only harm us, but had also caused confusion in the minds of people everywhere." Gorbachev continued: "We laid it out before the President this way .... I said I do not agree to his assessments of the human rights situation in the Soviet Union .... The facts that are mentioned do take place, but they are not yet the full picture of the Soviet Union."

According to Gorbachev's own account, the report continued, "he proceeded to upbraid Reagan over the human rights situation in the United States, to which Reagan objected." In the end, Gorbachev proposed the setting up of a lower-level working commission to pursue the issue, a proposal he expanded on in his June 1 press conference.[260]

Disagreement over the formulation of the term "peaceful coexistence" created an especially lively dispute between the two leaders at the last session of the summit. At their first private session Gorbachev proposed language for the closing joint statement that the President said seemed all right but thought it ought to be discussed with his aides. They found the language filled with Soviet code words, such as "peaceful coexistence," that might be interpreted to prevent the United States from continuing to press the Soviets harder on human rights violations and to support anti-Communist insurgents in the Third World. Accordingly, Soviet and American negotiators worked out a compromise in more noncommittal language.[261]

At the final formal session, the General Secretary directly challenged the President: "You said you were for peaceful coexistence. Then why not put [those words] in the communique?" Gorbachev asked the President's aides, "What about you, George [Shultz], Frank [Carlucci]? Why not this language?" After a five minute recess, the President, in the words of the account, "stood toe to toe" with Gorbachev and said quietly, "I'm sorry, this language is not acceptable." "Why not, Mr. President?" asked the General Secretary. "We can't accept it," the President replied without elaboration. "O.K. I can see I'm not going to change your mind," said Gorbachev, who quickly changed the subject.[262]

Soviet Deputy Foreign Minister Bessmertnykh gave a detailed account of the Soviet side of the dispute over the Studio 9 television program that provides another glimpse into the negotiations to resolve this issue. Bessmertnykh, who participated in this negotiation, believed that the exchange between the two leaders on this issue was "the crowning moment of the meeting." The following is the transcript of the television program giving his description of this negotiating encounter:

Mikhail Sergeyevich proposed: Why can't we, right now, on the basis of experiences gained through the four summit meetings, formulate a joint platform which would state such generally accepted norms as: Differences must be resolved through peaceful and non-military means. This is a direct political conclusion that stems from the concepts approved in Geneva; peaceful coexistence is the universal principle of people and states; everyone has the right to a political choice in social and economic spheres.

These strong, clear positions were offered to the President so that they could be jointly stated in a final document. The President immediately agreed. He said that he liked it, but he said, let us give it to the experts. But, as it happens, experts do not always make matters easier, at least, not all the experts. Therefore, when the last round of talks began in the Kremlin between Reagan and the general secretary, Mikhail Sergeyevich raised the question: What is your reaction to my proposal in this regard? Here is where the interesting discussion took place, first at the negotiating table. Mikhail Sergeyevich said: I see that you are not in agreement with each other. The President says one thing; George Shultz says something else, Carlucci says yet something else; Powell and Ridgeway say something else again. Maybe you should get together and consult amongst yourselves on the viewpoint you will accept. The delegates then parted. This took place in the Yekaterininskiy Hall. The American delegation retired to the opposite corner to give them an opportunity to consult with each other in private. After a while, they all got together again, and the discussion proceeded with the participants standing. After some tortuous talk, Reagan said: Mr General Secretary, unfortunately we cannot.

Our side presented arguments. We asked: Why the refusal? All right, we said, you do not agree with the concept of peaceful coexistence; let us put it differently. The people of the world are saying that there is a need to live in peace with each other. Are you against this? Perhaps you are against the right of people to social and economic self-determination or perhaps you are against the peaceful solution of disagreements. What is the matter? It goes without saying that the American delegation felt decidedly uncomfortable. Shultz said that they were uncomfortable with statements such as these and, therefore, requested that the matter be postponed for the time being.

Mikhail Sergeyevich then said: Well, we have stopped halfway through, but do give the matter some thought because this is truly a strong platform. If states as powerful as the USSR and the United States make public these future norms of behavior, then certainly it will create good, confident opportunities for normal development of events in world politics. This is one of the interesting episodes, and I think that although this discussion was not completed and was not expressed as a document, the mere fact that it took place, that people who formulate U.S. policies were present, will have great significance.[263]

All was not tranquil, therefore, at the Moscow Summit, particularly in the closed door sessions. The above dialogue, along with Gorbachev's press conference, suggest the intensity of the negotiations over outstanding differences between the two sides.[264] In a post-summit review, the President's advisors described scenes of "considerable tensions" between the two leaders, particularly over arms control matters. A good deal of tension was produced by Gorbachev, himself, who was said to be "extremely eager" to complete the strategic arms treaty as a decisive support for his internal reform campaign. In contrast, the President had no such internal pressures and hence could afford to pursue the negotiation more slowly and prudently.[265]

(c) Shultz on Summitry as a Negotiating Process. As for the actual roles played in the negotiations by the General Secretary and the President, Powell reported that the two principals did most of the talking in their face-to-face meetings, with contributions from Shultz, Carlucci, and himself, as well as Gorbachev aides.[266]

Secretary Shultz provides this instructive insight into the organization and functioning of the Moscow negotiations that suggests the evolution of this process into a creative international forum. In a Moscow interview aired over the MacNeil/Lehrer NewsHour on May 31, 1988, the Secretary gave this response to a query regarding the actual process of negotiations at the summit level:

> There has been an evolution in the way of working at these problems that I think is quite interesting and seems to work out well. Here's what happens: we bring here, and the Soviets have here, all of the expert people who know about this subject — the negotiators from Geneva, the people who do the work in Washington and their counterparts in Moscow. When we started out, the President and the General Secretary had a one-on-one meeting. Shortly thereafter, I had one with Foreign Minister [Eduard] Shevardnadze; and at that meeting we had around us this great big bunch of experts on all kinds of subjects — on human rights subjects, on regional issues, on bilateral problems, on the range of arms control issues, not just START and SDI — and we established working groups. And while we have been having these various meetings, the working groups, who are technically very well qualified, have

been meeting themselves. Being in the atmosphere of the summit meeting, there is the potential for interaction up and down the line from the political level of decisions to the technical level, and that tends to give a stimulus. By and large, I think, in each one of the summit meetings we've made progress working that way and we've become increasingly confident that that's a good pattern.

Addressing the issue of "atmosphere" over "substance" at the Moscow Summit in response to the assertion of a Soviet official that at this conference atmosphere was regarded as "first importance, substance second," the Secretary provided this additional positive evaluation of summitry as a diplomatic process:

I think I would disagree with him in wanting to rate them, because I think there is always an interplay. That's the real point. If there's no worthwhile substance, the atmosphere doesn't mean much. And, at the same time, a good atmosphere can contribute to substance. So the real point is that there has evolved—and this is the big story, it seems to me—a greater maturity, a greater breadth in the relationship, a genuine willingness to discuss practically anything, and progress across the board. It's not a one-issue relationship. It's not an arms control relationship. It's got all four categories of subjects—human rights, bilateral issues, regional problems, and arms control issues—all in it. They all get discussed very extensively, and we've made progress across the board. That's the really important point.[267]

c. Outcome and Performance of Principals

(1) Positive Outcome. As noted above, the Moscow Summit was a mixture of successes and failures, ultimately with postponement of critical strategic arms control issues for a future agenda. A balance of outcomes cannot be struck with any certainty. Perhaps, the most that can be said, in sum, is that both sides came away with some gains and suffered some losses. In the words of Mrs. Reagan in another context, it seemed to be a "Mexican standoff," that is, a draw. The transcending gain was mutual commitment to continuing dialogue and a determination to move forward on the strategic weapons agenda.

(2) Gorbachev's Performance. (a) As a Political Personality and Diplomatic Negotiator. What can be said about the performances of both principals? It has become commonplace to describe Gorbachev as a dynamic, imaginative political leader; a "natural campaigner" in the populist manner; and a negotiator who is tough, impulsive, often impatient, skillful and highly resourceful.[268]

At 57, Gorbachev was probably approaching the peak of his career when he met the President at their last summit, driving relentlessly with almost a compulsive energy to strengthen his power position at home, while keeping his "new thinking" foreign policy initiatives dynamically unfolding abroad.

At the summit Gorbachev had shown himself to be a vigorous campaigner who could stage (and control) political events to his best advantage. The press conference was a classic example of how the General Secretary could play out this political drama, upon which the eyes of the world were fixed, as a real professional, putting the Soviet case always in the best light, criticizing the U.S. side in a laundry list of complaints that by implication contributed to failure, registering his own disappointments and frustrations, but all the while maintaining that delicate balance between criticism and praise in order to sustain his argument that the summit was a successful "major event" in superpower relations. A realist, he could temper his criticism that "more could have been achieved" with the mitigating observation that "politics is the art of the possible," suggesting the limits imposed upon leaders of nations by the realities of political life.[269] The contrast between the young, vigorous Gorbachev and the aging President was striking throughout the summit. Twenty years his junior, Gorbachev performed at the press conference "with verve," it was said, for 110 minutes and "eagerly tackled detailed questions on diplomatic and political strategy," while drawing a picture of Reagan "being unwilling or unable to respond to Soviet initiatives in these final months of office."[270]

As a person, Gorbachev demonstrated that he could be warm and friendly and emotionally engaged on the personal level, as, for example, when he walked with the President through Red Square, and holding a small child in his arms, invited him to shake hands with "Grandfather Reagan." But he could be diplomatically cool and distant, if amiable, as on the occasion when Reagan suggested in closing remarks before his departure that he considered Gorbachev a friend; the General Secretary smiled faintly. When the President asked the Soviet leader to sign the Time magazine "Man of the Year" cover about him, Gorbachev agreed. "But in neither case," reported Gary Lee from Moscow, "did he return the compliment."[271]

In contrast to the emotional displays of Khrushchev and Brezhnev at previous summits and even the freewheeling negotiating style of Gorbachev at Reykjavik, "This time," said one American Soviet specialist, "Gorbachev's every move seemed programmed and controlled," implying the orchestration of his behavior to counter the growing opposition within the Party.[272]

(b) Gorbachev's Relationship with Reagan. In retrospect, Gorbachev's relationship with Reagan during the summit seemed to be marked by a mixture of amiability, strained conviviality, frustration and annoyance, controlled anger when defending the Soviet human rights record, combativeness in negotiations and a strict formality characteristic of leaders during official state visits.

Presidential aides described scenes of "considerable tension" between the General Secretary and the President, especially in negotiations.[273] In describing the personal chemistry between the two, one official noted that Gorbachev took a "very vigorous, self-confident" approach in private meetings with the President. Most foreign leaders, even close friends like Prime Minister Thatcher, tended to defer to Reagan because of his age and stature, the official said. "But Gorbachev doesn't show any deference or respect, for his age or his position," he added. Howard Baker expanded on this characterization saying that the two men "speak very freely and they speak very frankly." At one point, the Chief of Staff said, "They were face to face and going at it pretty heavy until the end," referring to the dispute over the formulation of peaceful coexistence. As he said, at that point the two men "stood toe to toe."[274]

Gorbachev characterized his working relationship with the President as warm and constructive, yet he portrayed Reagan at times in what was described as "withering terms, suggesting that he regards the American President as a man with little command of detail and perhaps overly dependent on overly cautious underlings."[275]

Even when the President was generous in expressing his support for Gorbachev's reform program, the General Secretary's response seemed distant and cool, even at times resentful. In virtually every speech, notably the address to the Moscow University students, the President took care to compliment Gorbachev on the liberalization of Soviet society he had already achieved, though indicating that more had to be done. This was intentional. As one adviser said, the President "believes that without Gorbachev there wouldn't be any this" liberalization. Yet Gorbachev did not altogether appreciate the compliment and frequently voiced his resentment at this interference and sermonizing. By and large Gorbachev's reply to the President's pressure was described as "suave, if a bit patronizing: the aged President, he implied, does not understand how rapidly events are moving in the Soviet Union and is denouncing conditions of the past." Americans, said Gorbachev, "just do not know about the process of democratization in this country."[276]

Yet there were times when Gorbachev did show consideration for the President. According to one report, in the "battle of images," the President several times appeared "tired and disengaged to the point that Gorbachev felt obliged to come to his rescue and cut off reporters' questions before one of their private sessions." A "dozing" President had on other occasions presented an unfavorable portrait in contrast to Gorbachev who, a generation younger and looked it, appeared "constantly animated, bursting with ideas and emotions."[277] Nothing had to be said; the portrait spoke for itself.

(c) Gorbachev's Accomplishments. As in the past, Gorbachev demonstrated again that he is a skilled and tough negotiator, an accomplished diplomat, and a resourceful, astute politician. From his pre-conference interview with The Washington Post to the post-conference speech to the peace activists, the General Secretary pursued his agenda with singular determination, attending to the details of the negotiations and the important externalities, orchestrating the media and stage-managing public events to his advantage, conceding when further resistance would be counterproductive, but remaining firm on the essentials, as in the case of the strategic arms issue. Minimal progress was made on this issue, but the larger question of changing the President's mind on critical issues such as SDI and revising the ABM Treaty, thus removing an obstacle to the strategic arms agreement, failed. Nonetheless, the arms control discussions were considered constructive. Still, that outcome appeared to have been expected. As one leading Party official said at the time, "We did not really anticipate any response to the [nuclear] arms proposals we made during the summit," adding that some reply would be expected before the next round of Soviet-American negotiations opening in Geneva during July.[278]

Gorbachev also succeeded in advancing his own hidden agenda; namely, to strengthen his internal power position against conservative rivals in the Soviet leadership who were about to put him to a test at the upcoming 19th Party conference scheduled for June 28. Throughout the summit the General Secretary proved his mettle as a skillful political manipulator by successfully playing a delicate game: to criticize the United States, the President and his negotiators for their failure to seize the opportunity for progress in arms control and their insistence on playing the human rights theme, but not to the extent that the summit effort would be discredited. Overkill would have reflected badly on his own foreign policy position. In carrying out this delicately balanced political maneuver, the President probably made a significant contribution. As one observer in Moscow noted: "All signs were that the presence of Reagan in the Soviet capital and his warm endorsement of Gorbachev's plans for reforming Soviet economic and political life were helpful to the Kremlin leader."[279]

Moreover, the General Secretary succeeded in formalizing many of his initiatives into agreements — initiatives, one authority described as "impressive."[280] Many had been initiated at the Geneva Summit; others refined at subsequent negotiating encounters. Final action on the INF Treaty was a major accomplishment not only for the President but also for the General Secretary which he regarded as the first step in creating a nuclear-free world. Accordingly, except for critical arms control issues, such as, reduction of strategic arms by 50 percent and coming to grips with conventional arms in

Europe, the superpower agenda appeared to be all but exhausted. These difficult matters were deferred to the future.

Finally, Gorbachev would claim that the Moscow Summit was a triumph for his foreign policy of "new thinking." Though mindful of its failures, the General Secretary did not lose sight of the larger purpose of continuing the superpower dialogue which is essential to the success of his foreign policy. As he truthfully said at the President's departure ceremony: "I believe that both of us have every reason to regard this meeting and your visit as a useful contribution to the development of dialogue between the Soviet Union and the United States."[281]

That Gorbachev intended to pursue this course in the future was evident when asked whether he thought an early summit meeting with the next U.S. President would be useful, he replied emphatically, "I consider it indispensable, vital."[282]

(3) Reagan's Performance. (a) Negotiating on Two Fronts: At the Conference Table and in the Public Forum. Reagan's negotiating strategy was directed at two political arenas: The conference table with his one-on-one negotiating encounters with Gorbachev; and in the public forum with direct, personal contact with the Soviet people. Both approaches drew upon Reagan's specialized expertise as a longtime aficionado of negotiations and as a "natural campaigner" who genuinely enjoyed the art and practice of politics and bore graciously and enthusiastically its elementary demands for direct engagement with the popular masses. As Hugh Sidey, the noted journalist and observer of the presidency, characterized the President in an article based on a telephone interview at Spaso House:

> Reagan is also a preacher – or, perhaps, a traveling salesman. He believes that the mashed-potato circuit, and now the caviar circuit, is made for hustling. He came to Moscow firm in his intent to discuss human rights rather than wrestle with the details of arms control. And discuss he did. Partly this reflected his need to burnish his hard-nosed conservative credentials back home: there was worry that he seemed more glowing in his endorsements of Gorbachev than of George Bush. But mainly it was because Reagan enjoys being a missionary and a teacher.[283]

The President went to Moscow, apparently, not expecting to conclude a START agreement. Attempts by the Geneva negotiators and by Shevardnadze and Shultz in a May ministerial meeting failed to remove the obstacles obstructing agreement. Nor could the President's leading national security advisers resolve their differences, so that a cloud of foreboding doom hung over the pre-conference meetings in the White House. Leading officials held out little hope for success in Moscow.

Thus the President went to Moscow with essentially modest diplomatic goals. As Jim Hoagland of The Washington Post observed in an analysis of the summit from Moscow, "He carried no new dramatic proposals and had already discounted the chances of reaching agreement on a treaty on strategic arms reductions here."[284] Breakthrough in strategic arms was not anticipated, therefore, and the demands on the President as a negotiator were expectedly not very great.

The President's major effort, therefore, was to be directed in the popular arena; that is, to influence Soviet public opinion and to further his campaign for human rights. Again, in Hoagland's analysis addressing this point, "he came with a firm concept of the highly personalized role he intended to play and pursed it with tenacity. It was as much a texture as any specific outcome that he sought to create in this visit."[285]

The day-to-day account of the meetings described above elaborates on the content and direction of the President's campaign in the public forum. In brief, it was a reassertion of the principles inherent in the Jeffersonian-Wilsonian tradition of democracy—the humane and promise-fulfilling values of human rights, the appeals of democracy as a force for economic growth and intellectual regeneration, the assurance of seeking peace through democracy, and the liberating effects of expanding democracy as a competing political philosophy in the world arena. Reagan hoped to impart these beliefs to his Soviet audience, for as he told Hugh Sidey, with respect to his address to the Moscow State University students (described as "moving and eloquent"): "That was very encouraging," said the President in a "surge of enthusiasm." He continued:

> Their interest was genuine. When I finished talking to the Soviet students, I met with 35 American students who are studying at the university. I can't believe this interrelationship does not affect governments. That's why I want to set up a program for more exchange, for thousands of students.[286]

The President's "relentless lecturing on human rights" sometimes "jangled Soviet sensibilities," and they complained. But a defensive Reagan remarked seemingly in feigned innocence on his performance, "I did not want to kick anybody in the shins. . . . I didn't think anything I said was too harsh."[287]

One aspect of the President's appeal was his determination to accent the positive not only in negotiating encounters with Gorbachev but also in the public forum—he came to praise Gorbachev, not to denigrate him. A review of the published sources during those 10 days of summit diplomacy suggests that the President fully intended "to take the high road," so to speak, of political persuasion, applying his verbal and visual skills as a master communicator. Symbolic of this direction was the occasion when the President presented Gorbachev with a copy of the film "Friendly Persuasion," a film about building reasonable, friendly relationships in a setting of discord and war—a metaphor for what he and the General Secretary were trying to do in Moscow. As for the President's ability to project a positive image over Soviet television and thus communicate his message more persuasively, perhaps Tom Shales' judgment has a special value. According to this much respected, nationally syndicated television critic, the President came across "at his warmest and best" over Soviet television.[288]

(b) On Dealing with Gorbachev: The "Prospero Factor" and the Burden of Age. Throughout the entire summit Reagan projected a positive and supportive view of Gorbachev. Never once did he publicly voice any direct, personal criticism of him. Like Gorbachev, the President, too, had a very difficult, sensitive and delicate task. He had to praise Gorbachev's reform, while making it clear that reform had much further to go; and he had to sharply criticize Soviet human rights performance, but without personally attacking or indicting the General Secretary. The delicacy of this task was especially revealed in his meeting with the university students where he struck a fair balance sheet on human rights but extended his appraisal to underscore the importance of institutionalizing reforms achieved thus far to insure durability. Reagan accomplished this task with deftness and candor, and objectively without giving undue offense to his Soviet host. Accordingly, the President placed the burden of such failures, as in emigration, on the Soviet bureaucracy, carefully protecting the General Secretary. And before the writers and intellectuals he went to great lengths to praise the General Secretary for loosening cultural constraints, giving him the ultimate compliment of acclaiming his "vision" as a leader.

Both the President and his aides made it clear that he and Gorbachev had "good chemistry," a phrase emanating from previous summits and stressed with increasing frequency. As he said to Hugh Sidey, "There is good chemistry between us," noting that this harmony was responsible for generating the progress achieved thus far. "I think that through this succession of summits," he continued, "there is a much better understanding," and referring to the Moscow meeting specifically added, "I think we made gains this time."[289]

When asked by foreign journalists on the occasion of being invited to the Gorbachev's private residence whether he considered Gorbachev a "real friend," the President replied: "I can't help but say yes to that. We can debate and we disagree. . . but. . . there is never a sense of personal animus when the arguments are over."[290]

And at Guildhall he gave this positive appraisal to his British audience: "My personal impression of Mr. Gorbachev is that he is a serious man seeking serious reform. We look to this trend to continue. We must do all that we can to assist it." [291]

Accordingly, the President could look back on his meeting with Gorbachev in a positive reflection. To reporters at Spaso House he said before departing that the "personal relationship" between himself and Gorbachev and between Soviet and American senior officials has "continued to deepen and improve." This relationship of good feeling, he implied, had much to do with producing a "good deal of important" work at the summit.[292]

Notwithstanding these positive appraisals, Reagan had to deal with Gorbachev with some serious disadvantages. The primary disadvantage was the age factor. At 77, and thus beyond the third quarter of life, the President was a full generation older than the 57-year old Gorbachev. Reagan's political life was nearing an end, while Gorbachev's was in the ascendancy. In Reagan this age disparity had the advantage of fostering what could be called the "Prospero factor," that is, the time in life when a person, like Prospero in Shakespeare's "Tempest," is winding down to a final close of life (like Shakespeare himself at the time he wrote this his penultimate play) which inspires a desire for reconciliation, a seeking of peace with adversaries — putting one's house in order before the end, so to speak. Many times in the second administration Reagan and those about him, especially Mrs. Reagan, expressed the desire of his leaving an historical record of peace and accord with the Soviet Union. It cannot be discounted that this desire was one of the many objective factors in bringing Reagan and Gorbachev together. Thus, the President, besides having a lifetime of political experience to bring to bear, could and did seize available opportunities to negotiate peaceful solutions to longstanding problems with his Soviet adversary. Metaphorically, the President was determined in the twilight of his second administration to leave the "house" of Soviet-American relations "in order" before his departure from the official scene, a fitting legacy for his successor and a memorable record for history.

Beyond this, the President's age was clearly a burden in the negotiations. Howard Baker was concerned for the President's health and stamina, although Reagan's fatigue was never a factor in the summit proceedings. "He is tired," said Baker at the end of the summit, "I guess he looks tired." Other officials who viewed Reagan up close during the summit said his energy and attention span had varied widely. At times he seemed sharp, replying quickly to Gorbachev's points, they said, but at other times his mind clearly seemed to wander and during one meeting he was observed dozing.[293] It was a tired president who "dozed" not only at the Bolshoi performance (to be awakened by a gentle tap from Gorbachev) but also during the meeting with the Soviet intellectuals.[294]

Most striking as a revelation of the impact of the age factor was the contrast between Gorbachev and Reagan at their respective press conferences.

Gorbachev performed "with verve" for 110 minutes and "eagerly tackled detailed questions on diplomatic and political strategy."[295] Reagan performed for 40 minutes evincing noticeable fatigue and sometimes confusion. Gorbachev showed off his alertness and managing skills in one instance by directing Soviet reporters to change seats with the Americans when a problem developed in the translation equipment. "Perestroika in action," said the report on the incident.[296]

In contrast, the President appeared very tired. As Steven Roberts reported, "He appeared fatigued by the four-day summit talks, and his aides acknowledged that the experience had been exhausting for him."[297] Upon returning to Washington, the President himself admitted twice in his welcoming remarks to being "tired," but was "exhilarated," nonetheless, by what had been accomplished.[298]

In a voice "frazzled with fatigue," said one report,[299] the President in his press conference revealed that he could not compete with "the control of material and snap of delivery" exhibited by Gorbachev (though he had often been acclaimed for his unique skill in communicating by reading long speeches and statements with great effect, a task deadly for most public figures but a skill he had developed to an art over his years as an actor). The President's prepared statement was described as coherent and his answers about dissidents and SDI "earnest and purposefully non-confrontational." But he declined to be drawn into details (perhaps out of deference to Gorbachev on the human rights issue and to his own preference to avoid details as, according to longtime observers, "a big picture man"). After a few questions, one account said, "fuzziness set in"; he drifted into "peculiar anecdotes about official bureaucracies and the American homeless." "Mercifully," it was said, "the questions were soft and the press conference brief. A kind fadeout." For this reporter, Walter Goodman of The New York Times, the President revealed a "mixed image" at the press conference. "There is nodding off at a writer's union lunch and looking rather vacant, almost stunned, beside the bright and vigorous Soviet leader," wrote Goodman, commenting on other incidents. Referring to the press conference, he rendered this final judgment: "the camera, which has been so kind to Mr. Reagan for so long, has turned cruel."[300]

Finally, Reagan had the disadvantage of being a "lame duck" President. In the twilight between a closing old administration and an incoming new one, the Presidency characteristically loses energy and practical leverage on shaping events, for in the transition power declines, expectations are reduced and possibilities fade. Gorbachev and his aides were well aware of this deficiency, and so could and did press the President hard for concessions on strategic arms knowing his vulnerability on the one hand and his desire on the other to conclude his second administration on a high point of superpower agreement.

(c) Reagan's Accomplishments: Stability and Continuity in Relations and Advancing the Cause of Human Rights. Reagan's primary accomplishment at Moscow was described as continuing the process toward establishing a "stable, sustainable" relationship and strengthening the Soviet-American dialogue for the future, a goal he had pronounced in the White House departure ceremony at the beginning of his Moscow trip.[301] To be sure, not all the items on his agenda were resolved, but, as Gorbachev said of the summit as a whole, that shortcoming can be attributed to politics being what they are, "the art of the possible."

Perhaps, General Powell came closest to explaining the importance of the Moscow meeting. In a post-summit briefing he expressed the belief that a "fairly stable, maturing relationship" had been established in Soviet-American relations and "will continue regardless of what the administration is." "We cannot allow this relationship to be governed by when this administration ends and the next one begins," he reasoned, and continued, "We are moving beyond individual problems to a broader discussion of systemic differences." "You don't make any sudden turns," he cautioned, "you just let it grow at a natural pace."[302]

Reagan's second major accomplishment at Moscow was seen as advancing the cause of human rights, a goal he had long professed as central to his political purposes. Again, as he reminded his listeners on leaving for Moscow, his second objective, similarly voiced on the eve of the Geneva Summit, was "to advance the cause and frontiers of human freedom."[303] Thus, according to a number of observers, he achieved his goal.

Reagan reached out to the Soviet people in general and to the various political and intellectual elites in particular with the verve of a "natural campaigner" driven by an unfailing belief in political democracy and human rights. He voiced special concern for the Soviet women who have borne a heavy burden in Soviet society, a gesture that was warmly received.

Reagan's basic message was one of human rights, freedom, and democracy. Thus on returning home the President declared that, "The biggest thing about this visit, the thing that impressed me the most, was the people." To them he sought to "explain America and what we are all about."[304] Exhilarated by great optimism for the Soviet-American future, he said that the summit had produced "a sense of hope, a powerful hope" for improvement in Soviet-American relations. But the "greatest significance of what took place," he said, was his opportunity to talk "words of faith, words of freedom, words of truth" directly with the Soviet citizens.[305] During this meeting, he said in another setting, "the seeds of freedom and greater trust were sown," and "I just have to believe that, in ways we may not be able to guess, those seeds will take root and grow."[306]

What the President's visit signified to many observers was his remarkable transformation from a "right-wing" political ideologue in the days of the "evil empire" to a realistic, pragmatic political leader and campaigner for human rights (which also received short shrift in the first administration). As one observer noted, "Ronald Reagan's mere presence here — if not his words — seemed to represent repentance."[307]

Gorbachev, himself, made special note of the Reagan transformation, indicating that Soviet-American relations were entering a new phase psychologically as a result. "I, myself, heard the President" say that his criticism of the Soviet Union as an "evil empire" belonged to "another time, another era," Gorbachev said proudly as he recounted his walk with Reagan through the Kremlin grounds. Reagan made the statement "within the walls of the Kremlin, next to the czar's cannon right in the heart of that evil empire," Gorbachev continued. "We take note of that. As the ancient Greeks say, everything flows, everything changes," adding, "One must be ready to look facts in the face. This is real politics."[308]

"This champion of anticommunism, who once roared against the Soviets' 'evil empire,' seemed tamed this week," reported Robert G. Kaiser of The Washington Post from Moscow at the close of the summit. The President left Moscow, he wrote, with a declaration that he and Mikhail Gorbachev had "slayed a few dragons" as allies fighting together against "threats to peace and to liberty."[309] For Reagan the linkage between human rights, perestroika and "new thinking" in Soviet foreign policy that brought improvement in Soviet-American relations was firm and inescapable: Human rights was the first cause.

There is an historical irony here akin to that occurring with other American leaders of the past whose presidencies ended finding them holding positions directly opposite to those initially taken: In his first administration Reagan publicly held Moscow in contempt as an "evil empire," ready to be consigned to the "ash heap of history," and relegated the human rights issue to a low priority; eight years later he made peace with this "evil empire," encouraged the success of its reformist leader, and openly professed that human rights was the principle of salvation for all humanity, including the Soviet Union.

Explanations for Reagan's transformation are no doubt many and varied but one, drawing upon his interview with Hugh Sidey, suggests that the President has an intuitive feeling for the larger course of history, the roles assigned by history to Great Powers and the freedom of choice available to leaders who will act — a notion of intuitiveness as being a type of assimilative intelligence of the world about him, a distinctive characteristic of leadership not always perceived by critical observers who tended to underrate his ability and insight. Having strengthened the Nation militarily following the Churchillian dictum, "arm to parley," and having found in Gorbachev a willingness to negotiate, the President was prepared to reach political solutions of their problems and establish a larger accommodation beginning with the Geneva Summit. With respect to the meeting in Moscow, Sidey continues,

> There is something so personal about this summit, the President explains. Systems may be brutish, bureaucrat may fail. But men can sometimes transcend all that, transcend even the forces of history that seem destined to keep them apart. The idea that he would ever go to Moscow was only a dim possibility until he met Gorbachev. Then it sprang to life in an intimate inkling at Geneva when they exchanged invitations for state visits as they walked from the pool house to rejoin their respective staffs.[310]

Thus, Sidey concludes, when history looks back, the Moscow Summit may prove to be "Reagan's finest hour, not to be measured by the treaties and agreements signed, because they were of modest nature, but by the easing of tension and the nurturing of understanding between the suspicious superpowers." According to Sidey, a longtime student of the presidency, Reagan had "defined the presidency in more detail and feeling during the Moscow Summit than he has ever done," and, he concludes, "He was making a bid for history to look up and take notice."[311]

A similarly favorable assessment of the Moscow Summit and Reagan's role in it was made by Evgeniy Primakov, a prominent Soviet foreign policy specialist and adviser to Gorbachev. He judged the Moscow meeting to be a "retreat" from the Cold War. But he cautioned, not all the barriers have been erected nor all the guarantees established to make sure that "the unfavorable and negative processes cannot occur again." Reporters had tried to provoke the President into making some unfavorable remarks about the Soviet Union—"to make him criticize us," he said. But the President "would have none of that and here Reagan as a political leader came to the fore." Primakov concluded with this admonition and appraisal: "one should not close one's eyes to the fact that he is a great political leader."[312]

C.   ESSENTIAL MEANING OF THE MOSCOW SUMMIT: AFFIRMATION OF DIPLOMACY AND NEGOTIATIONS

Thus, three essential points could be made with respect to the Moscow Summit. The conference was not a "turning point" in Soviet-American relations. Rather it was the consummation of a development in Soviet-American relations that began at Geneva in 1985; it symbolized the transformation in President Reagan's attitudes towards the Soviet Union; and it reaffirmed and justified Gorbachev-Reagan policies that sought superpower accommodation. In brief, the Moscow Summit was the culmination of a trend in

Soviet-American relations that put in perspective the record of eight years of a relationship that began in a state of aggravated stress and tension and ended with some promise and hope for the future. In this sense the Moscow Summit is a statement of faith in the value of diplomacy and negotiations.

D.   A POSTSCRIPT

No fifth-Gorbachev-Reagan summit was ever held in the post-Moscow period. Differences over strategic arms control could not be resolved during the remaining months of the Reagan Administration; the task was passed on to the incoming Bush Administration.

Relations gradually proceeded to wind down as the United States entered the fall presidential election and, after that, the usual political hiatus between administrations. Meanwhile, Gorbachev kept up his diplomatic offensive on a global scale. He made a major speech in Krasnoyarsk in Soviet Siberia on September 16, in which he expanded his peace initiative and sketched out a peaceful Soviet role as an Asian-Pacific rim power. On December 7, he addressed the United Nations, laying out his proposal for deep cuts in conventional arms in Europe. A "get-acquainted" meeting was held on Governor's Island in New York Harbor in the shadow of the Statue of Liberty between Gorbachev, Reagan and President-elect George Bush on the occasion of the General Secretary's visit to the U.N.

But beyond that formality there were no significant developments in Soviet-American relations. Clearly, Gorbachev was preparing for Reagan's successor, and on the U.S. side, the new Administration, though a "friendly takeover" by the same political party, had much preparation to do before specifically pursuing Soviet-American relations. New positions had to be filled, and policy reviews on a global scale had to be undertaken.

Thus for all practical purposes, the Moscow Summit was the final appearance on the world stage for Ronald Reagan, and for Mikhail Gorbachev it was the beginning of an entr'acte, a period of relations-held-in-abeyance until a successor Administration was firmly in place.[313]

Notes

INTRODUCTION

1. U.S. Congress. Committee on Foreign Affairs. Soviet Diplomacy and Negotiating Behavior, 1979-88: New Tests for U.S. Diplomacy. Study prepared by Dr. Joseph G. Whelan, Senior Specialist in International Affairs, Senior Specialists Section, Office of Research Coordination, Congressional Research Service, Library of Congress. Washington, U.S. Government Printing Office, August 1988, 876 p. (Special Studies Series on Foreign Affairs Issues, Vol. II. Committee Print.)

CHAPTER 1

2. Quoted in, Caldwell, Lawrence T. Washington and Moscow: Tale of Two Summits. Current History, v. 87, October 1988: 06. (Underscoring added).

3. For a discussion of this shift in the relationship, see, House Foreign Affairs Committee, Soviet Diplomacy and Negotiating Behavior, 1979–1988, chapter XII.

4. The Economist, v. 307, May 28, 1988: 23.

5. Goldman, Stuart D. U.S.-Soviet Relations. Washington, Foreign Affairs and National Defense Division, Congressional Research Service, Library of Congress, December 16, 1988, p. 6. (CRS Issue Brief: IB89008).

6. Shipler, David K. Reagan Will Go to Moscow for Summit Meeting May 29; Outlook on Arms Unclear. The New York Times, March 24, 1988, p. A1.

7. House Foreign Affairs Committee, Soviet Diplomacy and Negotiating Behavior, 1979–1988, p. 738.

8. *Ibid.* and Roberts, Steven V. U.S. Continues Pre-Summit Sparring with Soviets. The New York Times, April 26, 1988, p. A8.

9. House Foreign Affairs Committee, Soviet Diplomacy and Negotiating Behavior, 1979–1988, p. 738.

10. *Ibid.*

11. Barringer, Felicity. Soviet Warns Reagan Not to Meet Dissidents. The New York Times, May 27, 1988, p. A8.

12. *Ibid.*

13. *Ibid.*

14. *Ibid.* and Roberts, Steven V. Of Human Rights and Deadly Arms. The New York Times, May 27, 1988, p. A8.

15. The New York Times, May 27, 1988, p. A8. The Christian Science Monitor editorialized that the upcoming summit should not be "shrugged off" as Gorbachev's "going-away bash" for President Reagan. "That would be a mistake," for, as it explained, "the summit process is valuable in its own right. And the weight accorded this meeting should be based more on the reams it speaks about the evolution of attitudes shaping U.S.-Soviet relations than on the tonnage of signed documents." (A Summit With Substance. The Christian Science Monitor, May 26, 1988, p. 15.)

16. Roberts, Steven V. U.S. Aides See Summit Pomp, Not Substance. The New York Times, May 22, 1988, p. 1 and 12.

17. Gordon, Michael R. Outlook for Summit: Not Much Chance of Breakthrough on Arms Accord. The New York Times, May 26, 1988, p. A12.

18. The New York Times, May 22, 1988, p. 12, and Cannon, Lou and Don Oberdorfer. Reagan Off Today for Summit That Could Refurbish Presidency. The Washington Post, May 25, 1988, p. A24.

19. Saikowski, Charlotte, Menu of Bilateral, Regional Issues Awaits Summiteers. The Christian Science Monitor, May 25, 1988, p. 36.

20. The New York Times, May 22, 1988, p. 1.

21. The Christian Science Monitor, May 25, 1988, p. 36.

22. Saikowski, Charlotte. High-powered U.S. Team Goes to Moscow. The Christian Science Monitor, May 27, 1988, p. 34.

23. Quinn-Judge, Paul. Arms Cuts Top Soviet Wish List. The Christian Science Monitor, May 27, 1988, p. 1 and 34.

24. For a discussion of the impact of arms control on other aspects of Soviet-American relations, see, HFAC, Soviet Diplomacy and Negotiating Behavior, 1979–1988, p. 791–793.

25. The New York Times, May 26, 1988, p. A12.

26. Goldman, U.S.-Soviet Relations, p. 6.

27. The New York Times, May 26, 1988, p. A12.

28. Smith, R. Jeffrey. No Strategic Proposals Due at Summit. The Washington Post, May 25, 1988, p. A23.

29. *Ibid.*

30. The Christian Science Monitor, May 27, 1988, p. 1 and 3.

31. The New York Times, May 28, p. 1.

32. The New York Times, May 22, 1988, p. 12.

33. The Christian Science Monitor, May 25, 1988, p. 3 and 6, and May 27, 1988, p. 1 and 3.

34. The Christian Science Monitor, May 27, 1988, p. 34.

35. The Christian Science Monitor, May 25, 1988, p. 6.

36. The Christian Science Monitor, May 27, 1988, p. 36.

37. Goldman, U.S.-Soviet Relations, p. 13.

38. Havenmann, Judith. President's Visit to Moscow to Resemble Gorbachev's Here. The Washington Post, May 21, 1988, p. A21.

39. The Christian Science Monitor, May 27, 1988, p. 34.

40. The Christian Science Monitor, May 25, 1988, p. 6.

41. The Christian Science Monitor, May 25, 1988, p. 6, and The New York Times, May 22, 1988, p. 12.

42. Goldman, U.S.-Soviet Relations, p. 11-13.

43. The Washington Post, May 22, 1988, p. A1, A29–A34. Participants in the interview were: Katharine Graham, chairman of the board of The Washington Post; Richard Smith, editor in chief of Newsweek; Meg Greenfield, editorial page editor of The Washington Post and Newsweek columnist; Jim Hoagland, associate editor and chief foreign correspondent of The Washington Post; and Robert G. Kaiser, assistant managing editor for national news of The Washington Post and former Moscow correspondent. The transcript was prepared by The Washington Post from the original English and Russian language used during the interview.

44. *Ibid.*, p. 32.

45. *Ibid.*

46. *Ibid.*

47. *Ibid.*

48. *Ibid.*

49. *Ibid.*

50. *Ibid.*, p. A31.

51. *Ibid.*

52. *Ibid.*, p. A33.

53. *Ibid.*

54. U.S. Department of State Bulletin, v. 88, August 1988: 1–2.

55. For text, see Department of State Bulletin, August 1988, p. 2–6.

56. *Ibid.*, p. 4.

57. *Ibid.*, p. 7–8.

58. Roberts, Steven V. For Summit Planners, Image Counts. The New York Times, May 15, 1988, p. 14.

59. Kempe, Frederick and Peter Gumbel. Reagan Aims to Give Soviet Chief a Boost in Meeting at Summit: Gorbachev Needs a Success to Further "Perestroika" Within Communist Ranks. The Wall Street Journal, May 27, 1988, p. 1 and 10.

60. The Washington Post, May 25, 1988, p. A24.

61. Toth, Robert C. U.S. Firm on Soviets, Reagan Assures Allies. The Los Angeles Times, May 25, 1988, p. 1 and 14.

CHAPTER II

62. Department of State Bulletin, August 1988, p. 2.

63. FBIS Trends, May 27, 1988, p. 1.

64. Cannon, Lou and Gary Lee. President Opens Talks in Moscow. The Washington Post, May 30, 1988, p. A1. See also, Roberts, Steven V. reagan and Gorbachev Begin Summit Parley in the Kremlin; "Strike Sparks" on Rights Issue. The New York Times, May 30, 1988, p. 1 and 6; and FBIS-SOV-88-104, May 31, 1988, p. 7–8. This special publication by FBIS also contains the interview with President Reagan by Soviet television special correspondents Valentin S. Zorin and Boris Kalyagin, aired over Soviet television on May 28, but previously recorded in the White House prior to the President's departure for Moscow. See, p. 3–7.

65. Moscow Tass in English, 1111 GMT, May 29, 1988 and Pravda, May 30, 1988, 1st edition, p. 1, in FBIS-SOV-88-104, May 31, 1988, p. 8–9.

66. *Ibid*. See also the State Department Bulletin, August 1988, p. 8–9.

67. *Ibid*., p. 9–10.

68. Taubman, Philip. Reagan Presses Gorbachev on Church and Civil Rights; "Sermonizing" Annoys Host. The New York Times, May 31, 1988, p. A1 and A14; and Facts-on-File, June 3, 1988, p. 393.

69. Moscow Tass in English, 1407 GMT, May 29, 1988, in FBIS-SOV-88-104, May 31, 1988, p. 11.

70. The New York Times, May 30, 1988, p. 6. For a report from the Soviet side, see, Moscow Tass in English, 1734 GMT, May 29, 1988, in FBIS-SOV-88-104, May 29, 1988, p. 12.

71. Moscow Tass in English, 0521 GMT, May 30, 1988, in FBIS-SOV-88-104, May 31, 1988, p. 12.

72. Dobbs, Michael. The Matlocks: For Reagan's Hosts, the Week of Culmination. The Washington Post, May 29, 1988, p. B1 and B6.

73. The New York Times, May 30, 1988, p. 1 and 6, and Keller, Bill. Presidential Stroll: Chaos and Applause. The New York Times, May 30, 1988, p. 1 and 8.

74. *Ibid*. See also, Dobbs, Michael. Reagans' Sudden Stroll Sparks Fracas. The Washington Post, May 30, 1988, p. A1 and A22.

75. Facts-on-File, June 3, 1988, p. 394.

76. The Washington Post, May 30, 1988, p. A21.

77. *Ibid*.

78. *Ibid*.

79. The New York Times, May 30, 1988, p. 6.

80. Moscow Tass in English, 2111 GMT, May 29, 1988, in FBIS-SOV-88-104, May 31, 1988, p. 12.

81. Moscow Tass in English, 1030 GMT, May 30, 1988, in FBIS-SOV-88-104, May 31, 1988, p. 12.

82. The New York Times, May 31, 1988, p. A14. When asked by journalists what he thought about the President's plan to meet later in the day with dissidents, Gorbachev responded, "I don't know. We're currently meeting in this hall," adding, "We have the impression that we and you do not see the realities in this complicated problem quite well." Asked whether the leaders would discuss the list of 14 human rights cases presented to him by Reagan on Sunday, Gorbachev said, "There are too many lists." The President artfully dodged questions regarding his meeting with the dissidents, seeming to put the best face on an event that was displeasing to his host.

83. The New York Times, May 31, 1988, p. A14.

84. Department of State Bulletin, August 1988, p. 10–11. For a straightforward Soviet account of the visit to the Monastery, see Moscow Tass in English, 1137 GMT, May 30, 1988, in FBIS-SOV-88-104, May 31, 1988, p. 14–15.

85. Facts-on-File, June 3, 1988, p. 394, and The New York Times, May 31, 1988, p. A14. For an analysis, see, Roberts Steven V. A Mighty Pulpit for Reagan, Ibid.

86. Department of State Bulletin, August 1988, p. 11–12. For Soviet coverage of the President's meeting with the dissidents and refuseniks, see Moscow Tass in English, 1251 GMT, May 30, 1988, Moscow World Service in English, 1300 GMT, May 30, 1988, and Moscow Tass in English, 1147, May 30, 1988, in FBIS-SOV-88-104, May 31, 1988, p. 15–16.

87. Dobbs, Michael. Soviet Peace Committee Gives Hero's Welcome to U.S. Activists. The Washington Post, May 3, 1988, p. A11.

88. Oberdorfer, Don. At the Summit: Movement on Arms, Standoff on Rights. The Washington Post, May 31, 1988, p. A1 and A12.

89. *Ibid.*, p. A12.

90. *Ibid.*

91. Department of State Bulletin, August 1988: 12–13. For press coverage, see The New York Times, May 31, 1988, p. A1 and A14, and The Washington Post, May 31, 1988, p. A1 and A11.

92. Department of State Bulletin, August 1988, p. 13–15, and The New York Times, May 31, 1988, p. A14.

93. Taubman, Philip. Gorbachev Voices Irritation at Slow Pace of Missile Talks; Reagan Impresses Soviet Elite. The New York Times, June 1, 1988, p. A1 and A15.

94. Oberdorfer, Don. It's "Moscow Spring," Says Reagan. The Washington Post, June 1, 1988, p. A1 and A30.

95. *Ibid.*, p. A30. For other comments by Gorbachev see, Moscow Tass in English, 1012 GMT, May 31, 1988, in FBIS-SOV-88-105, June 1, 1988, p. 17.

96. Moscow Pravda, June 1, 1988, 2nd edition, in FBIS-SOV-88-106, June 2, 1988, p. 1.

97. In his phone interview with Hugh Sidey, the President said: "George Shultz told me about Red Square. I wanted to see it. I asked the General Secretary if he could take me by for a look, and when we went there we had that little walk. I was very impressed by the size and expanse of the square. And there were several groups of people out there, and we stopped to talk with them. Here, too, they were so warm and enthusiastic, just like all the others I had met in the city." Reagan did not visit Lenin's tomb because the line was long and he did not want to interrupt it. (Time, June 13, 1988, p. 14.)

98. The Washington Post, June 1, 1988, p. A30.

99. Cannon, Lou. Russians, Reagan: A Sizing Up. "It's Better to See Once than to Hear 100 Times." The Washington Post, June 1, 1988, p. A31.

100. The Washington Post, June 1, 1988, p. A30.

101. The Washington Post, June 1, 1988, p. A30. For Soviet coverage of the walk through Red Square, see FBIS-SOV-88-105, June 1, 1988, p. 8–15.

102. *Ibid.*, p. 10–11.

103. *Ibid.*, p. 14.

104. Facts-on-File, June 3, 1988, p. 395. This sentence was not produced in the Soviet source.

105. Moscow Domestic Service in Russian, May 31, 1988, in FBIS-SOV-88-105, June 1, 1988, p. 17–18.

106. Keller, Bill. The Vintage Actor Gets Great Reviews. The New York Times, June 1, 1988, p. A1 and A13. For excerpts from the President's address, see p. A12.

107. Remnick, David. Reagan Cites Roll Call of Cultural Icons. The Washington Post, June 1, 1988, p. A30.

108. Roberts, Steven V. President Charms Students, But Not by Dint of His Ideas. The New York Times, June 1, 1980, p. A13, and Lee, Gary. Students Find Reagan a Pleasant Surprise. The Washington Post, June 1, 1988, p. A30.

109. Department of State Bulletin, August 1988, p. 15–19. During the question and answer period, the President commented on changes in the youth of today, noting the "growing sense of responsibility that young people have"; responded to an inquiry on regional problems, emphasizing the goal of self-determination of peoples; addressed the problems of limitations of the President to two terms which he believed interfered with the democratic rights of the people; and addressed the historic problem of the American Indians, explaining its complexity. (For excerpts from the President's

speech and the question period, see The New York Times, June 1, 1988, p. A12.)

110. The New York Times, June 1, 1988, p. A13.

111. *Ibid.*

112. The Washington Post, June 1, 1988, p. A30.

113. *Ibid.*

114. *Ibid.* Helen Hanga, a 23 year old recent graduate of the university and now a Soviet journalist, explained the importance of this audience: "The future thinkers and activists are there. That's why it's important that Reagan speak there and try to make a good impression. A lot of the future of our country is there."

115. The New York Times, June 1, 1988, p. A14. The guest list, toasts and menu are reproduced in this source.

116. State Department Bulletin, August 1988, p. 21–22.

117. State Department Bulletin, August 1988, p. 22–23.

118. The New York Times, June 1, 1988, p. A1 and A15.

119. Moscow Television Service in Russian, 0755 GMT, May 31, 1988, in FBIS-SOV-88-105, June 1, 1988, p. 15–16. For Gorbachev's remarks at the ceremony and other coverage, see p. 17.

120. Gordon, Michael R. U.S. and Soviet Union Approve 9 Minor Accords. The New York Times, June 1, 1988, p. A1 and A15.

121. *Ibid.*, p. A15.

122. *Ibid.*. and Facts-on-File, June 3, 1988, p. 395.

123. The New York Times, June 1, 1988, p. A1 and A15.

124. Saikowski, Charlotte. Summitry Spurs Arms Control. The Christian Science Monitor, June 1, 1988, p. 1.

125. *Ibid.*, p. 32.

126. *Ibid.*

127. *Ibid.*

128. *Ibid.*

129. *Ibid.*

130. *Ibid.*

131. Observers Roundtable. Moscow Domestic Service in Russian, 1130 GMT, May 29, 1988, in FBIS-SOV-88-105, June 1, 1988, p. 35 and 37.

132. Oberdorfer, Don. Summit Brings Better Ties But No Arms Breakthrough. The Washington Post, June 2, 1988, p. A1.

133. *Ibid.*, p. A24.

134. Moscow Tass in English, 0836 GMT, June 1, 1988, in FBIS-SOV-88-106, June 2, 1988, p. 13–14. For Soviet coverage of comments by Gorbachev and Reagan to the press prior to this final meeting, see p. 12–13.

135. Department of State Bulletin, August 1988, p. 23–25. For the Soviet version as carried over Soviet television and as edited by Pravda, see FBIS-SOV-88-106, June 2, 1988, p. 14–15.

136. Time, June 13, 1988, p. 13.

137. Department of State Bulletin, August 1988, p. 25.

138. This summary is taken from the full text of the joint statement that was published in the Department of State Bulletin, August 1988, p. 25–31. For the Soviet publication of the text, see Moscow Tass in English, 1538 GMT, June 1, 1988, in FBIS-SOV-88-106, June 2, 1988, p. 16–22.

139. *Ibid.*, p. 26.

140. The Washington Post, June 2, 1988, p. A24. The Soviet draft and the final accepted statement are reproduced in this source.

141. *Ibid.*, p. 26–28.

142. *Ibid.*, p. 29.

143. *Ibid.*, p. 29–31.

144. Lee, Gary. "Missed Chances" at Summit. The Washington Post, June 2, 1988, p. A1 and A25.

145. Excerpts from Gorbachev's Press Conference. The New York Times, June 2, 1988, p. A18.

146. Taubman, Philip. Gorbachev Criticizes Reagan, Seeing "Missed Opportunities," But Calls Visit a "Major Event." The New York Times, June 2, 1988, p. A1.

147. The Washington Post, June 2, 1988, p. A1 and A25.

148. The Washington Post, June 2, 1988, p. A24.

149. The Washington Post, June 2, 1988, p. A25.

150. The New York Times, June 2, 1988, p. A18.

151. The Washington Post, June 2, 1988, p. A25.

152. *Ibid.*

153. The New York Times, June 2, 1988, p. A18.

154. *Ibid.* For the Soviet text of the Gorbachev press conference, see Moscow Television Service in Russian, 0927 GMT, June 1, 1988, in FBIS-SOV-88-106, June 2, 1988, p. 22–36.

155. For the text of the press conference, see the Department of State Bulletin, August 1988, p. 31–35.

156. Moscow Tass in English, 1503, GMT, June 1, 1988, in FBIS-SOV-88-106, June 2, 1988, p. 43; The New York Times, June 2, 1988, p. A17; and The Washington Post, June 2, 1988, p. A24–A25.

157. *Ibid.*

158. The Washington Post, June 2, 1988, p. A24.

159. Department of State Bulletin, August 1988, p. 35–36. For the Soviet text, see Moscow Television Service in Russian, 0609 GMT, June 2, 1988, in FBIS-SOV-88-106, June 2, 1988, p. 44–45.

160. Lee, Gary. Reagan Lauds Gorbachev in Farewell. The Washington Post, June 3, 1988, p. A1 and A26.

161. Department of State Bulletin, August 1988, p. 36.

162. The Washington Post, June 3, 1988, p. A1.

163. Moscow Tass in English, 0749 GMT, June 2, 1988, in FBIS-SOV-88-106, June 2, 1988, p. 45–46.

164. Facts-on-File, June 3, 1988, p. 396.

165. For the text of the President's address, see Department of State Bulletin, August 1988, p. 36–40. For a synopsis, see The Washington Post, June 4, 1988, p. A1 and A19.

166. *Ibid.*, p. A19.

167. *Ibid.*

168. Department of State Bulletin, August 1988, p. 40–41.

CHAPTER III

169. Roberts, Steven V. Summit Wasn't the World Series, U.S. Says, But Was Still a Success. The New York Times, June 3, 1988, p. A1 and A11.

170. FBIS Trends U.S.S.R.-U.S., June 8, 1988, p. 1. (FBIS 172.)

171. The Washington Post, June 2, 1988, p. A23.

172. FBIS Trends, U.S.S.R.-U.S., June 8, 1988, p. 1. (FBIS 172.)

173. Toth, Robert C. U.S. Firm on Soviets, Reagan Assures Allies. The Los Angeles Times, May 25, 1988, p. 1 and 14.

174. Cannon, Lou. Reagan Buoyed by Summit, Cautious on START. The Washington Post, June 7, 1988, p. A17.

175. Department of State Bulletin, August 1988, p. 9.

176. *Ibid.*, p. 31.

177. *Ibid.*, p. 14.

178. McAllister, Bill. Summit "Seeds" Will Grow, Reagan Says in Radio Recap. The Washington Post, June 5, 1988, p. A27.

179. Pravda, June 1, 1988, 2nd ed., p. 1 and 2, in FBIS-SOV-88-105, June 1, 1988, p. 13.

180. Department of State Bulletin, August 1988, p. 32.

181. FBIS Trends, U.S.S.R.-U.S., June 8, 1988, p. 1–2. (FBIS 172.)

182. Moscow Meeting: Successful Dialogue in the Interests of Confidence and Peace. Pravda, June 7, 1988, 2nd ed., p. 1, in FBIS 056, p. 1.

183. Moscow Television Service in Russian, 1700 GMT, June 5, 1988, in FBIS-SOV-88-108, June 6, 1988, p. 16–17.

184. Studio 9 Television Program on Moscow Summit. Moscow Television Service in Russian, 0350 GMT, June 11, 1988, in FBIS-SOV-113, June 13, 1988, p. 20–21.

185. Havenmann, Judith. Reagan Returns from Summit, Calls Meeting "Momentous." The Washington Post, June 4, 1988, p. A19.

186. *Ibid.*

187. *Ibid.*

188. Quinn-Judge, Paul and Charlotte Saikowski. A New Era of Cooperation: Superpower Relations Reach a "Higher Level." The Christian Science Monitor, June 2, 1988, p. 1 and 32.

189. Saikowski, Charlotte. Even the Pomp at Summit Signaled Significant Change. The Christian Science Monitor, June 6, 1988, p. 3–4.

190. A Summit to Build On. The Christian Science Monitor, June 2, 1988, p. 15.

(Editorial). The Washington Post praised the Moscow Summit, particularly the discussions on human rights and the caution exercised in concluding agreements before their time. "Summits make theater and occasionally they also make history," the Post said, " – and it is not unknown for them to make large misunderstandings and mistakes. We think it as well that the two principals did not try to hasten or force new accords for which there was not yet sufficient preparation or agreement. We are glad Mr. Reagan went to Moscow – and glad he is coming home without any unfortunate additional baggage." (Down from the Summit. The Washington Post, June 2, 1988, p. A20. Editorial.) A feature article in Time magazine concluded: "Exhilaration is perhaps too strong. The superpower leaders had merely got through a summit that produced no breakthroughs but no backsliding either. Given the angry animosity that for so long divided the U.S. and U.S.S.R., however, that is no small achievement. . . . Even when summits end without any breakthrough on arms control – even if, as Gorbachev said, they leave a vague sense of missed opportunity – the fact that they now seem almost a matter of course may, in fact, be the most amazing thing about them." (Time, June 13, 1988, p. 22.)

191. Seib, Gerald F. Last Hurrah: Entering the Stretch, Reagan Sees Summit as Start of New Drive. The Wall Street Journal, May 23, 1988, p. 1.

192. The New York Times, June 3, 1988, p. A1 and A11.

193. Gordon, Michael R. Hope, but No Promises. The New York Times, June 2, 1988, p. A1 and A17.

194. Goldman, U.S.-Soviet Relations, p. 6.

195. The New York Times, June 2, 1988, p. A1. For a discussion of START see, Caldwell, Washington and Moscow: A Tale of Two Summits, p. 307–308. For analysis and commentary on the issue of the SLCMs at Moscow, see Talbott, Strobe. The Summit's Good Soldiers: An Anatomy of the Arms-Control Impasse That Made the Difference, Time, June 13, 1988: 25. Bessmertynkh sums up the Soviet view of these negotiations in his appearance on Studio 9 television program on June 11, 1988. He notes that the draft text of the START agreement, currently under study, as "a thousand or so" brackets. "A bracket means that there has not been an agreement as yet on a certain point," Bessmertynkh states. "Of the thousand or so brackets, only five or so are key issues. The solution of these would immediately lead to elimination of the remaining brackets." Of all these, he notes, "the

most important one is the question of adherence to the ABM Treaty as it was signed in 1972." (FBIS-SOV-88-113, June 13, 1988, p. 21.)

196. The New York Times, March 24, 1988, p. A1.

197. The New York Times, June 2, 1988, p. A16.

198. The New York Times, June 4, 1988, p. 6.

199. The New York Times, June 2, 1988, p. 17 and June 4, 1988, p. 6.

200. The Washington Post, May 22, 1988, p. A31.

201. The New York Times, May 23, 1988, p. A13.

202. Roberts, Steven V. U.S. Continues Pre-Summit Sparring with Soviet. The New York Times, April 26, 1988, p. A8.

203. Department of State Bulletin, August 1988, p. 5.

204. Gertz, Bill. U.S. Bargained Hard in Moscow. The Washington Times, June 23, 1988, p. 1.

205. The Economist, v. 307, May 28, 1988: 23.

206. Roberts, Steven V. U.S. Aides See Summit Pomp, Not Substance. The New York Times, May 22, 1988, p. 1.

207. Roberts, Steven V. For Summit Planners, Image Counts. The New York Times, May 15, 1988, p. 14 and The Washington Post, May 21, 1988, p. A21.

208. This section is based mainly on, Cannon, Lou and Don Oberdorfer. The Scripting of the Moscow Summit. The Washington Post, June 9, 1988, p. A29 and A34.

209. The Washington Post, June 2, 1988, p. A28.

210. FBIS-SOV-88-113, June 13, 1988, p. 26.

211. This section is based on, Gerstenzang, James and Michael Parks. U.S. Government Run from Soviet Capital: 5,000 Miles from Potomac, White House is in Business. The Los Angeles Times, June 1, 1988, p. 12; The Economist, May 28, 1988, p. 23–24; and Time, June 13, 1988, p. 27.

212. The Los Angeles Times, June 1, 1988, p. 12.

213. *Ibid.*

214. *Ibid.*

215. According to one official, the delegation was severely limited, "because the Embassy in Moscow can just hold so many people." "It's very difficult, very cramped working conditions," he added. "More people want to go on this trip than if we were going to Ouagadougou. It's amazing how many people think the President couldn't function without them." (The New York Times, May 22, 1988, p. 12.)

216. *Ibid.*

217. Facts-on-File, June 3, 1988, p. 394.

218. The Christian Science Monitor, May 27, 1988, p. 1 and 3.

219. Saikowski, Charlotte. High-powered U.S. Team Goes to Moscow. The Christian Science Monitor, May 27, 1988, p. 1 and 34.

220. Studio 9 Television Program. Moscow Television Service in Russian, 0350 GMT June 11, 1988, FBIS-SOV-88-113, June 13, 1988, p. 24.

221. For an appraisal of the Soviet foreign policy infrastructure, see, HFAC, Soviet Diplomacy and Negotiating Behavior, 1979–88, chapters IX and X.

222. Time, June 13, 1988, p. 25.

223. The Washington Post, June 3, 1988, p. A27.

224. Victory for Realism and Reason. CPSU Central Committee General Secretary's Special Representatives Brief Foreign Statesmen. Pravda, June 8, 1988, 2nd ed., p. 6, in FBIS-SOV-88-177, June 17, 1988, p. 4.

225. Studio 9, in FBIS-SOV-88-113, June 13, 1988, p. 23.

226. Time, June 13, 1988, p. 22.

227. Shales, Tom. Media Glasnost, Soviet Savvy. The Washington Post, June 1, 1988, p. B1.

228. Remnick, David. Moscow's Leap Into the Media Age. The Washington Post, May 31, 1988, C1 and C4.

229. The Washington Post, May 31, 1988, p. C4.

230. Time, June 13, 1988, p. 22.

231. The Washington Post, June 1, 1988, p. B1 and B10.

232. Time, June 13, 1988, p. 22.

233. The Washington Post, June 1, 1988, p. B1 and B10.

234. The Washington Post, May 31, 1988, p. C4.

235. FBIS. Special Memorandum. Soviet Treatment of President Reagan's Speeches at the Moscow Summit, June 24, 1988, p. 1. (FB88-10008). See also, FBIS Trends, U.S.-Soviet Summit Portrayed as Major Success, June 8, 1988, 2 p. (FBIS 172).

236. Lee, Gary and Robert G. Kaiser. Public Impressed; President "Stands Up Well to Everyone." The Washington Post, May 31, 1988, p. A11.

238. The Washington Post, June 1, 1988, p. A33. A U.S. official said that the denunciations of Roshko and several other guests were "an obvious attempt to cast a shadow over an event that had a lot of appeal in this country." He did not deny the Soviet allegations made against Roshko but said that the Soviet Union and the United States have actively traded information about Nazi war criminals "and they have never once before mentioned Roshko, even though we have brought his case to them" for an exit visa.

239. See, HFAC, Soviet Diplomacy and Negotiating Behavior, 1979–1988, Chapter IV.

240. The Washington Post, June 1, 1988, p. B1.

241. The Washington Post, June 1, 1988, p. A31.

242. Keller, Bill. Veil on Personalities is Pulled Aside. The New York Times, June 2, 1988, p. A19.

243. The Washington Post, June 1, 1988, p. A31.

244. *Ibid.*

245. Barringer, Felicity. First Ladies' Travelling Road Show: We're Fine, Thank You Very Much. The New York Times, May 30, 1988, p. 8.

246. *Ibid.*

247. *Ibid.*

248. Facts-on_file, June 3, 1988, p. 385 and Time, June 13, 1988, p. 18.

249. Radcliffe, Donnie. Nancy vs. Raisa: Round 2, First Ladies' Gallery Give-&-Take. The Washington Post, June 2, 1988, p. C2.

250. *Ibid.*

251. The Washington Post, June 1, 1988, p. B1.

252. HFAC, Soviet Diplomacy and Negotiating Behavior, 1979–88, p. 63–67.

253. The Washington Post, May 26, 1988, p. A1.

254. The New York Times, June 1, 1988, p. A12.

255. The Washington Post, May 25, 1988, p. A24. (Underscoring added.)

256. Moscow Television Service in Russian, 1430 GMT, May 31, 1988, in FBIS-SOV-88-105, June 1, 1988, p. 11. (Underscoring added.)

257. The New York Times, May 31, 1988, p. A13.

258. The New York Times, June 3, 1988, p. A1 and A11; and The Washington Post, June 2, 1988, p. A23.

259. Lee, Gary. Gorbachev Seen as Adept at Summit. The Washington Post, June 5, 1988, p. A27.

260. *Ibid.* For the Soviet report on Gorbachev's speech, see Moscow Television Service; in Russian, 1751 GMT, June 2, 1988, in FBIS-SOV-88-107, June 3, 1988, p. 20.

261. Time, June 13, 1988, p. 22.

262. *Ibid.*

263. Studio 9, Moscow Television Service in Russian, 0350 GMT, June 11, 1988, in FBIS-SOV-113, June 13, 1988, p. 23–24.

264. One issue that generated antagonism on both sides was Nicaragua. Gorbachev had repeated an offer to end all but small-arms shipments if the United States would stop support for all governments in the region. U.S. negotiators rejected this proposition. According to one official, the General Secretary "gave no impression he was really interested in serious dialogue." He added that "the President indicated that continuing Soviet military support for Sandinista repression hindered effective U.S.-Soviet cooperation on regional issues." (Gertz, Bill. U.S. Bargained Hard in Moscow. The Washington Times, June 23, 1988, p. 1.)

265. The New York Times, June 4, 1988, p. 1 and 6.

266. The Washington Post, June 4, 1988, p. A19.

267. State Department Bulletin, August 1988, p. 20–21.

268. For an analysis of Gorbachev's political persona, see HFAC, Soviet Diplomacy and Negotiating Behavior, 1979–1988, p. 651–675. In a recent interview Gromyko made this commentary on Gorbachev's political abilities:

"I have been of the firm opinion, ever since I met Gorbachev long ago, that he is a man of sharp and profound mind, with great abilities and a correct understanding of our future tasks. That is why I spoke up for him at the Central Committee plenum, when the candidate for general secretary was being chosen." (The Observer, London, April 2, 1989, p. 21 and 23, in FBIS-SOV-89-062, April 3, 1989, p. 8.) In his speech Gromyko had referred to Gorbachev as a man with "iron" teeth suggesting his political toughness.

269. FBIS Trends, U.S.-Soviet Summit Portrayed as Major Success, June 8, 1988, p. 1 (FBIS 172). Gorbachev's realism and candor were recently demonstrated in a speech to Soviet workers on internal reform when he acknowledged with extraordinary frankness: "This open and direct exchange about our society, about the accumulated problems, initially flabbergasted everyone. I tell you, even we did not know everything—even those sitting next to you—not everything, and even now we do not know everything and understand what it is all about." (Moscow Television Service in Russian, 1800 GMT, February 14, 1989, take 2, FBIS 007.)

270. The Washington Post, June 2, 1989, p. A23.

271. The Washington Post, June 5, 1988, p. A27.

272. *Ibid.*

273. The New York Times, June 4, 1988, p. 1 and 6.

274. The New York Times, June 3, 1988, p. A11.

275. The New York Times, June 2, 1988, p. A19.

276. Time, June 13, 1988, p. 22.

277. *Ibid.*, p. 21.

278. The Washington Post, June 5, 1988, p. A27.

279. The Washington Post, June 2, 1988, p. A1.

280. Caldwell, Washington and Moscow: A Tale of Two Summits, p. 338.

281. State Department Bulletin, August 1988, p. 36.

282. Taubman, Philip. Summitry and Beyond. The New York Times, June 3, 1988, p. A1.

283. Time, June 13, 1988, p. 14.

284. The Washington Post, June 3, 1988, p. A23.

285. *Ibid.*

286. Time, June 13, 1988, p. 18, and The Washington Post, June 2, 1988, p. A23.

287. Time, June 13, 1988, p. 14.

288. The Washington Post, June 1, 1988, p. B10.

289. Time, June 13, 1988, p. 17 and The Washington Post, June 1, 1988, p. A31.

290. The Washington Post, May 21, 1988, p. A21.

291. The New York Times, June 4, 1988, p. 1.

292. State Department Bulletin, August 1988, p. 31.

293. The New York Times, June 3, 1988, p. A1 and A11.

294. Under the heading, "A friendly cue," Time noted: "Seated comfortably at the Bolshoi Theater, Reagan kept his head high, even while drifting off to sleep. One minute before the end, he felt a soft tap on his arm and heard a few English words from an interpreter. The President awoke with a chuckle in time to join the applause. The wake-up call had come from Gorbachev." (Time, June 13, 1988, p. 27.)

295. The Washington Post, June 2, 1988, p. A23.

296. Goodman, Walter. TV Coverage: Is the Camera Turning Cruel? The New York Times, June 2, 1988, A18.

297. The New York Times, June 2, 1988, p. A16.

298. The Washington Post, June 4, 1988, p. A19.

299. Time, June 13, 1988, p. 13.

300. The New York Times, June 2, 1988, p. A18.

301. The Washington Post, May 26, 1988, p. A1 and A17.

302. The Washington Post, June 4, 1988, p. A19.

303. State Department Bulletin, August 1988, p. 1.

304. Time, June 13, 1988, p. 14 and 17.

305. The Washington Post, June 7, 1988, p. A17.

306. The Washington Post, June 5, 1988, p. A27.

307. Thatcher, Gary. Reagan and Gorbachev Play to Mixed Reviews in Moscow. The Christian Science Monitor, June 2, 1988, p. 1.

308. The Washington Post, June 2, 1988, p. A23.

309. Kaiser, Robert G. Leaders Team Up Against Cold War Dragon. The Washington Post, June 3, 1988, p. A1.

310. Time, June 13, 1988, p. 17.

311. *Ibid.*, p. 18.

312. Vremya newscast. Primakov Interview by Viktor Lyubovtsev. Moscow Television Service in Russian, 1700 GMT, June 5, 1988, in FBIS-SOV-88-108, June 6, 1988, p. 17. Primakov had been impressed by the fact that the President listened closely to Soviet views rather than simply rejecting them during their one-on-one sessions. Another senior Soviet official said of Reagan: "The acting and the charm worked fine. . . . But the main thing is that beneath them there seemed to be a certain sincerity. In this country, people have a strong sense of sincerity and people feel it with Reagan." (The Washington Post, June 1, 1988, p. A31.)

313. For recent surveys of Soviet and U.S. policy during the Reagan years, see America and The World, 1988/89, Foreign Affairs, v. 68; Tucker, Robert W. Reagan's Foreign Policy, p. 1–27; Johnson, Paul. Europe and the reagan Years, p. 28–38; Holloway, David. Gorbachev's New Thinking, p. 66–81; Legvold. Robert. The Revolution in Soviet Foreign Policy, p. 82–98; and Zagoria, Donald S. Soviet Policy in East Asia: A New Beginning? p. 120–138.